P9-AQB-965

GUIDANCE MONOGRAPH SERIES

SHELLEY C. STONE

BRUCE SHERTZER

Editors

GUIDANCE MONOGRAPH SERIES

The general purpose of Houghton Mifflin's Guidance Monograph Series is to provide high quality coverage of topics which are of abiding importance in contemporary counseling and guidance practice. In a rapidly expanding field of endeavor, change and innovation are inevitably present. A trend accompanying such growth is greater and greater specialization. Specialization results in an increased demand for materials which reflect current modifications in guidance practice while simultaneously treating the field in greater depth and detail than commonly found in textbooks and brief journal articles.

The list of eminent contributors to this series assures the reader expert treatment of the areas covered. The monographs are designed for consumers with varying familiarity to the counseling and guidance field. The editors believe that the series will be useful to experienced practitioners as well as beginning students. While these groups may use the monographs with somewhat different goals in mind, both will benefit from the treatment given to content areas.

The content areas treated have been selected because of specific criteria. Among them are timeliness, practicality, and persistency of the issues involved. Above all, the editors have attempted to select topics which are of major substantive concern to counseling and guidance personnel.

Shelley C. Stone

Bruce Shertzer

THE INITIAL
COUNSELING
CONTACT

JOSEPH FRANCIS PEREZ

THE STATE COLLEGE, WESTFIELD, MASSACHUSETTS

HOUGHTON MIFFLIN COMPANY · BOSTON

NEW YORK · ATLANTA · GENEVA, ILL. · DALLAS · PALO ALTO

UNITY SCHOOL LIBRARY
Unity Village
Lee's Summit, Missouri 64063

DISCARD

COPYRIGHT © 1968 BY HOUGHTON MIFFLIN COMPANY. *All rights reserved. No part of this work may be reproduced or transmitted in any form or by any means, electronic or mechanical, including photocopying and recording, or by any information storage or retrieval system, without permission in writing from the publisher. Printed in the U.S.A.*

F
37
c6
744

CONTENTS

EDITORS' INTRODUCTION

It is unusual to find a whole book — even a small book — devoted entirely to a discussion of a single, brief meeting between two individuals. However, such is the purpose of this monograph. Through analysis, example, and concrete guides, the initial counseling contact is thoroughly examined in all of the complexity inevitable in the purposeful interaction between two individuals. The first counseling session is, as Dr. Perez so appropriately stresses, of utmost importance. The influence of initial impressions, the impact of first happenings on later sessions, and, indeed, the ultimate success or failure of a series of counseling contacts may be determined during the first crucial meeting.

The actual time spent in the initial contact between counselee and counselor is relatively brief, but despite this, what transpires is amazingly complex. Two unique individuals interact dynamically in a setting where one seeks professional help and the other attempts to provide it. Each participant enters the process with a complex psychological defense system, with a highly individualized perception of his life situation, with different ways of managing interpersonal relationships, and with his own motives for being in this specialized kind of situation. Each participant interacts with the other to determine the character of the first session and inevitably to influence all subsequent sessions.

Dr. Perez clearly discusses the counseling interaction occurring within the initial contact. He skillfully enriches his discussion with actual examples of counselor-counselee interchange which give life to his presentation. He provides highly readable material which contributes to an understanding of the counseling relationship in its early and critical stage.

The content of the monograph will be of equal value to both the experienced counselor and the novice because of its stimulating and thought-provoking character.

SHELLY C. STONE
BRUCE SHERTZER

AUTHOR'S INTRODUCTION

A first meeting is crucial. This assertion has been made by others (Arbuckle, 1961; Wolberg, 1954). It is crucial primarily because it results in a first impression which is well retained and quite difficult to erase. A first meeting between counselor and counselee is important, for if they find counseling mutually rewarding, the stage has been set for a therapeutic and satisfying series of sessions. If the participants find it unrewarding, however, there will be no subsequent interviews.

The general purpose of this monograph is to minimize the need for the counselee to do any later "erasing" of his initial impressions about you, the counselor. Or to state the same thing positively, the purpose here is to provide you, the counselor, with guides which will help you to experience successful first interviews. An equally important purpose of this monograph is to help you to conduct first meetings which will assist you to learn, interpret, and determine if you should have subsequent meetings with the counselee.

More particularly, the author's purpose here is to help you, the counselor (guidance person, social worker, psychologist, or physician), to conduct first interviews which are mutually rewarding and lead to additional productive contact between the participants.

J. F. P.

Dimensions of
the Initial Counseling Contact

The Point of View

Counseling is an interactive process, a process in which the counselor and the counselee are participants in an enterprise which has as its purpose helping the counselee to deal more effectively with reality. Reality includes all the people, objects, and situations which the individual receiving counseling perceives in his environment.

More particularly, the point of view taken here is that counseling brings together two personalities with uniquely separate dynamics. The dynamics for both are in general the same, but they may differ widely in the particulars. Thus, both counselor and counselee have the same needs: namely, to feel secure, to feel accepted, to feel worthy, and to achieve whatever measure of freedom they feel they can. Let us note, however, that the *degree* or *level* of security, acceptance, etc., will vary.

In addition, both counseling participants have a psychological defense structure. They may even utilize the same defenses. Counselor and counselee, however, vary as to how, when, and under what circumstances they use their defenses. The use of defenses on the part of counselor and counselee varies because their perception of the world varies. Thus, what the counselor may view as reward (a pat on the back, for example) the client may possibly view as threat (He's hitting me).

Perception, in turn, affects interaction. Therefore, how a client perceives the counselor and how the counselor perceives the client, of course, determine how the two individuals will relate to each other.

Meanings generally are derived from interaction. These meanings can be conscious or unconscious, cognitive and/or emotional. Meanings are crucial because they determine future perception. For example, the counselee who leaves his initial counseling contact with the thought, "I like the counselor," will be willing, if not eager, to return. On the other hand, the client who goes away with feelings of dislike — or, at best, mixed reactions — may never return.

In summary, both client and counselor are alike in that they are both human beings with dynamics (needs and defenses). Moreover, both perceive, interact, and derive meaning from the world. But, at the same time, they are quite different in that each will vary in need level, defense pattern, perception, mode of interaction, as well as quality and quantity of meaning derivatives.

Counseling has been variously categorized as vocational, educational, motivational, and personal. The point of view here is that *all* counseling is a personal process and must consider an individual's dynamic life. The author's conviction is that often a client's vocational, educational, motivational problems are basically a function of unsatisfied needs and/or an inadequate system of defenses.

Counseling is viewed throughout this monograph as an interpersonal experience; a process which brings together two unique personalities whose dynamics are in constant action and reaction; a process which is vitally concerned with such topics as rapport, technique, and communication.

Some Theoretical Concerns

Goals

The general topic of goals in counseling has precipitated a vertitable Niagara of comments, essays, and studies. Most authors of counseling theory have had something to say on the topic (Arbuckle, 1961; Perez, 1965; Rogers, 1951; Sullivan, 1954; Thorne, 1950; Williamson, 1950; and Wolberg, 1954). Although goals seem to be of vital concern to all types of professional counselors (Michaux and Lorr, 1961; Lorr, 1965), one researcher has found that goals vary with the individual counselor's perception of counseling (Poole, 1957).

This counselor believes that there is really only one goal for the initial interview, namely, to determine whether there should be subsequent interviews. It is only realistic to expect that sometimes additional contact will not occur. This may be due to any number of reasons: There may be an unfortunate clash between the participants' dynamics (needs and defenses); the counselor may feel that the client's problem is beyond the scope of his professional competence and training; the client's problem may need only one session, etc.

The Setting

There is research evidence that the attractiveness or shabbiness of one's surroundings can influence an individual's perception of people (Mintz, 1956; Maslow and Mintz, 1956). It may be inferred from these studies that the client's perception of the counselor, particularly in the initial contact, will be affected by where the counseling takes place. Moreover, assuming equality of counselor competence, it is fair to conclude from these studies that the counselor who functions in a bare, poorly lighted, shabby room is not likely to get as good results as one who works in an office which is well-lighted, adequately furnished, and generally attractive. In any case, whatever the counselor can do to make his physical surroundings more attractive will only aid him in making his counseling more successful.

Ordinarily, however, the problem of the initial counseling contact revolves not around the setting so much as it does around the first steps taken by both participants toward the development of the phenomenon termed "rapport."

The Question of Rapport

Rapport can be simply defined as a working relationship involving mutual warmth, trust, and confidence.

The reader should be fully aware that rapport is seldom achieved at the initial contact, no matter how great may be the zeal, affect, or competence of the counselor. The anxiety, fear, guilt, and resentment of the counselee more often than not are simply too strong to be dissolved in one session. At the first session, the counselor and client whether they are aware or unaware of the need for rapport) can be expected only to *begin* development of their "working relationship."

Rapport and Perception

The counselor can facilitate the achievement of rapport if he is aware of and seeks to understand the counselee's perception of reality.

The counselor who can communicate at the first session, if not a full understanding, at least an awareness and appreciation of the counselee's unique perception will move a long way toward insuring a successful first session; more important, he will provide a basis for subsequent sessions. At the first session, the counselor should strive to let the counselee understand and feel that "I, the counselor, know that you view the world differently than I; however, I would like very much to come to understand — and even share — your view of it."

There are two reasons why the counselor should strive to make this communication to the counselee. The first is a humane one. It serves to let the counselee know that he is accepted and respected just because he is a human being. [Such a communication does what Rudikoff and Kirk (1961) had in mind when they wrote that an "immediate goal" in counseling involves "mobilizing the counselee toward greater inner satisfaction."] Secondly, it is only through understanding the counselee's perception that the counselor can come to understand the counselee's mode of interaction, since — as noted above — an individual's interactions are, to a very great extent, a function of his perception.

Rapport and the Interactive Process

At the initial meeting, then, interaction between counselee and counselor should be directed toward creating a climate in which the counselee can begin to feel secure, accepted, worthy, and free. There are a number of things which the counselor can do and say to facilitate the development of such feelings in the counselee.

Goodstein and Grigg (1959) have observed that a counselor is, or at least should be, a real-life person, one who reacts to and interacts with the needs of the counselee. Such a person may be defined as a human being with emotions and feelings which he is continually seeking to attach beneficially.

Security

The counselee must feel secure to be himself. He must feel that he can express statements which he would not dare to express in many other, or even *any* other, places. He must feel safe enough to verbalize and release the fear, guilt, anxiety, resentments, and suspicions which beset him. This is particularly true during the initial contact when, as Rogers (1951) has observed, "attitudes being expressed are relatively superficial."

The counselee often harbors ideas which a part of him recognizes to be neurotic or even marginally psychotic. The tension which he experiences because of these ideas often becomes insurmountable. The counseling interaction should afford him the security to unbind, to verbalize the doubts, the fears, the guilt — and thereby to release the tension.

The following examples, appropriate and inappropriate, illustrate how a counselor may engender feelings of security and insecurity in the counselee:

CEE:* I'm afraid to go to French class.
    Appropriate responses by the counselor:
        Tell me about it.
        How long have you had that feeling?
        We all have our fears.
    Inappropriate responses by the counselor:
        Oh, silly (*chuckling*).
        Really now, I'll bet you yourself know how childish that is.
        You shouldn't feel that way.

CEE: I could have hit Miss Jones for saying that to me in front of all the kids.
    Appropriate responses by the counselor:
        Let's talk about it.
        I know what you mean.
        It's a very human feeling to have.
    Inappropriate responses by the counselor:
        My God!
        I'm sure you're bright enough to know what would have happened.
        We all have to learn to suppress such urges.

CEE: I know he doesn't really like me.
    Appropriate responses by the counselor:
        He doesn't like you?
        Why do you think that?
        Hmmm. How long have you felt this way?
    Inappropriate responses by the counselor:
        You don't really believe that.
        Don't be silly!
        I'm sure in your saner moments you're not so suspicious.

The reader will observe that the appropriate remarks, those which promote security, not only permit, but also encourage further expression of feeling by the counselee. The inappropriate remarks are threatening to the counselee, belittle him in most cases, or — worse still — only serve to cut off discussion.

Acceptance

The counselee must be made to feel that he is accepted, understood, and — more important — that he not only belongs to but is an integral part of the counseling process (Lorr, 1965). The counselor will find that tolerant, respectful comments, a warm affect, and facial expres-

---

* Hereafter, CEE and COR will be used to refer to Counselee and Counselor, respectively.

sions which communicate frankness and sincerity will go a long way toward promoting a feeling of acceptance in the counselee. Unlike Tarachow (1963), this author feels that the counselor should communicate friendliness from the first moment. Quite simply, if subsequent counseling does not occur, it should not be because the counselor was unfriendly. Also there is research which suggests that this position is probably correct. For example, Pohlman and Robinson (1960) found that counselor aloofness, insincerity, and lack of warmth only "displeased" counselees.

The following examples will help to explain how appropriate counselor statements can help the counselee to feel accepted and how inappropriate counselor statements can engender counselee feelings of rejection:

CEE: I don't know if I can make every Monday appointment.
>   Appropriate responses by the counselor:
>>   Let's discuss it.
>>   You can't make every Monday appointment?
>>   Perhaps we need to arrange a more flexible schedule.
>   Inappropriate responses by the counselor:
>>   Oh. That might pose problems!
>>   Oh, why not? You know, it might be difficult to easily arrange a different appointment day.
>>   Oh, no!!

CEE: I'm not very bright, am I?
>   Appropriate responses by the counselor:
>>   You don't feel you're bright?
>>   How long have you felt this way?
>>   Tell me what you understand by "bright."
>   Inappropriate response by the counselor:
>>   Well, don't worry about it.
>>   I don't know if you are or not.
>>   The tests indicate that you aren't in the upper half of your class.

CEE: I'm sort of worried about something. A lot of girls think I'm a pain.
>   Appropriate responses by the counselor:
>>   This bothers you.
>>   You don't feel that you are as popular as you'd like to be.
>>   Why don't we discuss it?
>   Inappropriate responses by the counselor:
>>   I wouldn't worry about it; worrying doesn't help.
>>   Well, you'll get over it, don't worry. A lot of people your age feel the same way.
>>   Maybe you could try a little harder with them.

Again, what the reader should note is that appropriate responses promote feelings of acceptance and encourage release of feelings; inappropriate responses tend to alienate, cut off, or, at best, discourage release of feelings.

Worthiness

The counselor should constantly strive to promote feelings of worth in the counselee; or, in Olsen's (1966) words: "The values held by counselors must be based upon a primary concern for the personal worth and dignity of each individual." A common reason for the counselee to seek counseling is precisely because he does not feel worthy, or put another way, his self-esteem is low.

A client who feels insecure or unaccepted is not likely to feel worthy. To a very great extent, an individual's performance in particular roles, or as a person, is a function of his self-esteem level. To feel worthy, then, is crucial.

The following examples illustrate how the counselor can raise or lower counselee self-esteem:

CEE: I'll never get into college. You see, I rank in the bottom quarter of my class.

 Appropriate responses by the counselor:

  You feel you won't be admitted because you haven't performed well enough.

  Shall we talk about it?

  Tell me about the subjects you've enjoyed so far.

 Inappropriate responses by the counselor:

  That's not so good, is it?

  Your concern is not unrealistic.

  Not everyone can go to college, you know.

CEE: I'm sorry I'm late again.

 Appropriate responses by the counselor:

  Would you like to discuss this lateness?

  You're sorry you're late.

  I wonder why you're late?

 Inappropriate responses by the counselor:

  This is you, I suppose.

  I wonder if you couldn't try a little harder to *do* something about it.

  Do you think you really want counseling?

CEE: I'm the only one in the room who got four 100%'s in French this term.

 Appropriate responses by the counselor:

  This makes you feel good.

> Très bien. Tell me all about it.
> The only person to get four 100%'s in French.
> Inappropriate responses by the counselor:
> We usually do well in subjects we like.
> French was my best subject in school, too.
> How many exams did you have?

Again, what the reader should observe is that the appropriate remarks are those which encourage expression of feeling and attitudes, and inappropriate remarks, those which discourage expression of feelings.

Freedom

Throughout the counseling process, and beginning with the initial meeting, the climate should be one of total freedom. Quite simply, the client should feel free to be himself, free to express his own particular brand of humanity, free not to have to conform to values, ideas, or ideals with which he is not identified or about which he is in conflict.

Without this freedom, the counselee could hardly hope to realize his best potential or, as Patterson (1963) has noted, "to become a responsible, independent, self-actualized person capable of determining his own behavior." According to Waskow (1963), it is the judgmental counselor who blocks feelings of freedom, who blocks the client's experience and expression of emotions.

The following are some illustrative examples of ways in which feelings of freedom in a counselee can either be promoted or discouraged:

CEE: A lot of kids cheat in the chem lab.
> Appropriate responses by the counselor:
> What's your reaction to that?
> How do you feel about it?
> Do you think cheating's a problem today?
> Inappropriate responses:
> Just so long as you don't do it.
> Isn't it awful?
> I don't know what's the matter with the kids today.

CEE: (*Chuckle.*) A lot of girls are drinking in the dorm.
> Appropriate response by the counselor:
> There's drinking in the dorm.
> What do you think about it?
> Why do you think that is?
> Inappropriate responses:
> They can get into a lot of trouble if it's discovered.
> Silly kids!
> Well, they won't last in college; they're not usually exactly the best students.

CEE: A lot of my friends are having premarital affairs.
         Appropriate responses by the counselor:
             Hmmm. Why do you think that is?
             You feel there are a lot of premarital affairs going on?
             What are your thoughts on it?
         Inappropriate responses:
             Well, there's always been some of that, I suppose; but today
             it's really a pretty bad situation.
             God!
             Don't worry. They'll pay for it, one way or another.

What we can observe in the above four sets of illustrations is that appropriate responses (those which promote rapport) are: (1) tactful, (2) respectful, (3) tolerant, (4) kindly, and (5) rewarding. Conversely, inappropriate responses are: (1) tactless, (2) judgmental, (3) intolerant, (4) unkind, and (5) punitive. To reiterate, appropriate responses promote and encourage expression of feelings; inappropriate responses cut off such expression. Finally, appropriate remarks are those which feed and elevate the needs of security, acceptance, self-esteem, and freedom. Inappropriate remarks lower, or at best threaten, these same needs.

The Question of Identification

For many a counselee, the initial interview is seen as an opportunity to obtain a model with whom to identify. The counselor is perceived by such a counselee not as a disseminator of information or a helper, but, according to Williamson (1966), as a "possible role model." This observation seems to find some support in a paper by Pepinsky and Karst (1964), who believe that client-counselor interaction is invariably characterized by "an amount of convergence which involves a measurable shift in client behavior toward that of the therapist."

This shift in client behavior quite probably occurs more readily with younger clients. Or, put more simply, adolescent clients probably need a model with whom to identify more than middle-aged clients. If one follows this line of thinking, it would seem that the high school counselor, particularly, should be aware of the client's need to identify. In any case, the point to be noted here is this: current psychological thought holds that the counselor serves as a likely identity model for many a counselee.

What does it mean if the client seeks to identify with the counselor? It may mean that the client feels that he can continue to grow by identifying with the counselor. It may mean that the client perceives traits, qualities, abilities, ideas, or mannerisms in the counselor which he wishes to incorporate into his own personality. It may mean, at the very least, that the client will follow and respond positively to most — if not all — counselor cues. And finally, it may mean that, if necessary, the client will return for subsequent counseling sessions.

How can the counselor know if the client seeks to identify with him? Ordinarily this is not difficult to perceive, for the client will use words, inflections, or mannerisms which are characteristic of the counselor before, during, and/or after counseling sessions. The client in such cases also expresses positive attitudes and feelings toward the counselor, toward counseling, toward psychology.

How will the counselee's need to identify affect the initial counseling interview? If the counselor is receptive, such a need should only facilitate the interview. Thus, the counselee's need to incorporate counselor traits and characteristics would seem to mean that the rapport and necessary communication should be easily achieved.

Should the counselor try to encourage or discourage identification? In light of the immediately preceding response, it would seem that the counselor should try only to encourage identification. How can he do this? Actually, there is little the counselor can do to encourage identification, for the need, ability, and willingness to identify lie within the need system of the counselee. At best, all the counselor can do is to be himself, to be his own professional person. If the counselee's needs lead him to perceive traits, qualities, etc., in the counselor which he finds attractive, then, in all likelihood, he will demonstrate his need to identify.

Now, what if the situation is reversed? What if, at the initial interview, the counselor perceives qualities and traits in the counselee which appeal strongly to him? In other words, what if the counselor seeks to identify with the client? There is little harm for anyone if the counselor incorporates an occasional client quality. There is considerable harm, however, if the counselor seeks to identify with many qualities of successive clients. Such a counselor has little sense of his own identity and should not counsel.

But what if the counselor simply likes the client? What does this mean? How will this liking affect the initial counseling interview?

There are clients whom the counselor will like and others whom he will not like as much. There may even be some whom he will dislike. (Hopefully, these will be few.) If the counselor is attracted toward a counselee, he will naturally find it easier to establish rapport; and he will be even more favorably disposed toward meeting the client's needs, i.e., security, acceptance, self-esteem. There is research which appears to substantiate these thoughts, for Stoler (1963) concluded from a study in client likability that "It is possible that the therapist may be unable to provide effective therapy to a client he cannot like." It is reasonable to infer, then, that liking the client can only facilitate and promote a successful first interview.

The Question of Structure

Structuring refers to communicating (either verbally or affectively) to the counselee what he may realistically expect to occur in counseling. Structuring also involves letting the counselee know what the roles and responsibilities of the participants are. As noted above, the client comes into counseling with all sorts of feelings, fears, guilts, resentments, and, often, suspicions. One of the purposes of structure is to allay these feelings.

Counselors vary in their positions about structure. Tolbert (1959) sees a need for it, since it expedites client learning about what he can expect to occur in counseling. Both Thorne (1950) and Wolberg (1954) believe in it firmly and believe also that it is the counselor who should supply it. The former states that ". . . the responsibility for determining the counseling method . . . depends upon the counselor." Wolberg states that counseling "time will have to be spent in structuring the therapeutic situation, expounding on the process [what counseling is] in very simple language." Non-directionalists Rogers (1951) and Arbuckle (1961) believe that any structuring which occurs must emanate from a position of mutual involvement or from the attainment of what Rogers calls the "unified perception" of counselor and client. Structuring by the counselor, they feel, may block client involvement and interfere with the satisfaction of his needs. An article by Tyler (1956) also supports the latter position.

Following are three examples of structuring. The first one illustrates a rather rigid, pro-structure, counselor-in-control-of-the-situation position.

Example One

COR: This is our first meeting now. . . . We've spent quite a while talking, and I'm afraid I haven't made it clear what's going to happen here. I think you made it clear you want to see me. (*Pause.*) (*Chuckle.*) You *do* want to see me?

CEE: Oh, yes!

COR: Fine. I think you should know that in counseling it is you who is going to determine what happens. That is, we have to cooperate with each other. We'll be talking about your attitudes towards books and school and Miss Jones. You do some more thinking about these things, and when you come back next — Uh, when can you see me again?

CEE: I don't know. Uh — I'm free third period on Tuesday and Friday.

COR: Fine. You come back next Tuesday at 11:15 and we'll go over your attitudes; we'll review what you feel your attitudes are. Then, maybe we'll be able to get at some of your true feelings toward Miss Jones and why you can't get along with her. Do you understand?

CEE: I think so. I'll talk about what I think about things, and that'll help me understand myself better.

COR: Yes, I hope so. But you understand we can't guarantee anything. We can only hope that you'll have a better understanding of yourself in relation to school and Miss Jones. I'm here to help you understand yourself better. If you cooperate — (*trailing off*)

CEE: By talking about how I feel about her.

COR: Yes.

CEE: O.K. I get the picture.

There is no doubt as to who is in control. The counselor runs the session. He has explained in a strong but not-unkind way what the counselee is to do and what he can expect to happen, noting even that ". . . we can't guarantee anything."

Example Two

This second example illustrates a considerably more moderate position than that in the preceding example. It still reflects clearly, however, a counselor attitude that the client must have a realistic expectation of what is to occur and that he understands the roles and responsibilities of both parties:

COR: So, what do you think counseling's all about?

CEE: I don't know. I suppose I talk and stuff.

COR: You talk. Right!

CEE: Yeah.

COR: About what. I mean —

CEE: (*Giggle.*) I talk about how I feel about my (*chuckle*) reason for being here, my husband.

COR: Yes, about your relationship with him.

CEE: Yeah. (*Pause.*) And what do *you* do?

COR: I listen. I'll talk some. Mostly I'll listen.

CEE: And what will that do?

COR: I hope (*chuckle*) I'll be able to clarify, help you understand how you feel about him and other things.

CEE: Hm-m-m-m.

[PAUSE]

Will things be better for me — I mean, after?

COR: If we get along, you and I, and I think we will, I think you'll see things better. I think you'll feel better.

CEE: Well, I never expected any miracles. This sounds all right. Good. So, when can I see you again?

Cor: Uh, let's see. What's more convenient, mornings or afternoons?
Cee: Afternoons.
Cor: I'm free Mondays at 2:00 and 3:00 and Thursday at 3:00.
Cee: Monday's O.K.
Cor: Good. Monday at 2:00. That's your hour.

This counselor is considerably less controlling than the last, but is still quite persistent, even insistent, that the counselee understand her role and responsibilities, and that, if they "get along," the client should come to feel better and see things more clearly.

Example Three

This last interview is an example of a counselor who is not especially concerned with structure as defined here. This counselor is more concerned with focusing on client-counselor relationship, with how they view each other, with how they get along:

Cee: Well, we've been talking for almost an hour.
Cor: Yes. How do you feel about this first hour?
Cee: Well, I guess I needed it badly. It's so seldom you can get to talk to anybody. I mean, you know, talk like about people in this college. God. (*Pause.*) I needed it!
  [Pause]
Cor: You feel a little relieved.
Cee: Yes, I suppose I do. I feel relieved.
  [Pause]
  I've always liked psychology.
Cor: Uh-huh.
  [Pause]
Cee: Yeah. (*Pause.*) Yeah, and I always kinda wondered what went on here at the counseling center.
Cor: Now you know.
Cee: Now I know.
  [Pause]
  It's really good, this — (*trailing off*).
Cor: This what?
Cee: This counseling business.

This counselor was the least controlling of the three. His focus was not to structure, but rather to clarify for both himself and the client, the nature of their relationship. His prime concern was more to engender in the client feelings of security, acceptance, worthiness, and freedom than to communicate mutual roles and responsibilities.

Views on Structuring

Whether or not the counselor structures the interview is going to be dependent on his own and the client's need states, defense patterns, and general perceptions. Let us note that there are counselors who function optimally only if they can structure, manipulate, and direct the course of counseling (Example One above). And let us note that these counselors function — if not well — at least satisfactorily. In any case, there are clients who continue to see them. Whether or not these clients derive significant meaning from the interaction is difficult to determine.

There are counselors, too, who within the framework of their clearly structured situation focus on the client's needs, defenses, and perceptions. These counselors may also make a significant contribution (Example Two above). Finally, there are counselors who are unconcerned with structure as a theoretical topic and, at best, view it as of only utilitarian value. Structure, these last feel, should not be a focal point in the initial contact or, indeed, at any point in the counseling process. The concern should be the *relationship,* and any structure issued is incidental and, equally important, arrived at by mutual consent and motivation (Example Three above).

The author's position on structure lies somewhere between Examples Two and Three above; more simply, the belief here is that counseling is an interactive process, and its prime purpose is to meet the client's needs — not those of the counselor. The conviction here is that the counselor who can communicate this to the counselee will quickly develop the rapport conducive to the relationship sought by the counselor in the third example above.

Structuring, then, should not emanate from the counselor's needs, as is true in Example Two, but rather from the counselee's needs. For example, many individuals seek counseling because of difficulties with authority figures. The author submits that a counselor necessarily casts himself in the role of an authority figure (and this is particularly true on initial contact) when — without solicitation — he explains roles, responsibilities, and even expectations. This is not to deny that there are counselees who may need structure, for there are. Those counselees who have learned to be suspicious, who want to know what "this counseling business" is all about, should be told. The counselor's prime concern, however, remains the counselee's needs, *not* his own.

The Question of Communication

There is little doubt among exponents of counseling theory that communication is *a,* if not *the,* central issue in the counseling process (Patterson, 1959; Perez, 1965; Rogers, 1961; Thorne, 1950; Williamson, 1959). Of course, the level (verbal simple, verbal complex, or behavioral) and the extent to which communication will take place is determined by the dynamics of the counseling participants. With the possible exception of the client who is authoritatively referred (i.e., via the principal's office), the assumption may be made that the counselee *wants* to communicate. For, more often than not, it is precisely his inability to communicate with people which has led him to seek counseling. Despite this, it should be understood that in many cases, perhaps most, the counselee will be in conflict about expressing and releasing his thoughts, feelings, and dissatisfactions. To do so, he has found, may be punitive or, at best, unrewarding. It then becomes dependent on the counselor's dynamics whether or not counselee conflict can be sufficiently abated to promote communication between participants. As has been noted elsewhere (Patterson, 1959; Perez, 1965), the counselor himself may be a barrier to effective communication.

A counselor will not be able to work effectively if his needs state is so insatiable, or his defense patterns in such a state of malfunction, that he simply cannot become effectively attuned to the counselee's needs and defenses. The point of view here, then, is that a counselor's ability to communicate is dependent not only on the nature of his dynamics and those of the counselee, but also on the nature of the interactive process achieved by the two. Buck and Cuddy (1966) are apparently of the same opinion, since they have observed ". . . that the meaning of a communication is initially tied to the nature of the relationship between the participants."

Communication in counseling, as in life in general, may occur verbally (simple or complex) or behaviorally — or in a combination of these. The counselor whose dynamics permit him to utilize each of these modes of communication will be more successful than one who is dynamically blocked from utilizing one or more. An important counselor goal at the initial interview, then, might be to communicate to the counselee that the latter is free to relate on the verbal level (simple or complex) and on the behavioral level as well.

Simple Verbal

Verbal communication can be simple or complex. Let us consider the simple verbal communication first. Simple verbal communications are easy to follow, because there is little, if any, emotional blocking. The counselee who chooses the simple verbal means of communicating is ordinarily in relatively good health. Such a counselee chooses words which are simple, not emotionally charged, and which do not have subjective meaning. The counselee who can communicate at this level is generally one whose perception is accurate and whose mode of interaction has proved rewarding for the most part.

An example of communication at the simple verbal level follows. The counselee is a female, eighteen years old, and a high school senior. The setting is a school psychologist's office:

CEE: I'm here. I don't want to be, but I am.

COR: Yes, (*chuckle*) I see.

CEE: Mr. Jones [the principal] sent me.

COR: I know.

CEE: Look. It's all kinda silly. I mean, so I threw an eraser at another girl; it was a friend of mine. I mean, for heavens sake! Big deal. I don't need counseling.

COR: You don't need counseling.

CEE: No. I mean really! Next year I'll probably be married. Just because I threw an eraser at Ginny, does that mean I have to see a psychologist? I mean, I'm not a nut or anything. It was in fun. She threw one at me first. It's just that I got caught by Miss Kevin. She wasn't feeling good again today.

COR: You don't think that just because you threw an eraser at another girl you need to be seen in counseling?

CEE: Right. This school is starting to give me the creeps. I mean really! You throw an eraser back at a friend and they send you to the psychologist!

COR: You don't like being in here just for throwing an eraser.

CEE: Well, no; I don't. I mean, I'm a good student. I've never even been in detention in four years of high school, and suddenly I find myself here. I mean really! Do you really think I need to be, to be counseled, I mean honest, do you?

COR: What do you think? What do you feel?

CEE: No, 'course not.

COR: I see.

CEE: So. So, will you please sign the pink slip, so I can go back to class.

COR: (*Chuckle.*) Yes, of course.

The above illustrates a not-uncommon occurrence in the public high schools. The counselee suddenly finds herself in counseling because of acting out in a good-natured, playful way. All her comments are made easily, simply, and to the point. Moreover, her background of four years without detention lends considerable objective evidence that this is not a girl with serious interpersonal problems.

Complex Verbal

Verbal communication can also be quite complex. More often than not, the complexity stems from the counselee's emotional confusion which interferes with his ability to choose words which communicate adequately his thoughts and feelings. Often, a counselee's verbalizations reflect his need for long-term help. The counselee's words, a function of subjective and indigenous feeling, quite understandably have meanings which are commensurate to these feelings. Very often, the counselee has developed a uniquely unhealthy perception of the world. Quite understandably, his interactions are therefore in terms of his perception and, consequently, unrewarding. His feelings, a product of constant frustration, anxiety, and punishment, are confused — and so is his choice of words. It devolves upon the counselor, then, to be exquisitely sensitive, not only to the words, but also to the feeling tones behind and attached to the words.

Following is an example of counseling dialogue which may be termed *complex verbal*. This counselee is a female, twenty-three years old, and a college senior. This is the initial contact:

(1) CEE: Yeah, I know a,a, a lot of kids who've been here [the counseling center].

[PAUSE]

They seem to think that — Well, I don't know what they think; really, who really knows what they or anybody is thinking these days.

(1) COR: We're all of us really quite alone when you come down to it.

(2) CEE: Yeah. That's for sure. Sometimes when I'm alone . . . alone . . . God. How awful it is at night, at night in the dorm. I could scream. Four walls — partitions — partitions between people. There's something between all of us. Something's standing, all the time, something's up all the time between me and people. People, God, who needs 'em? They scare me, they disgust me. Who knows about them? I don't know. Maybe that's why I'm so conscious of partitions between me and people.

(2) COR: You feel there are barriers between you and others.

(3) CEE: Exactly.

[PAUSE]

(3) COR: The dorm makes you feel —

(4) CEE: Alone. (*Pause.*) The dorm . . . the dormitory. I mean a place to sleep, you know. Comes from Latin. (*Pause.*) I never sleep. Sleep. There's a passage in Shakespeare about sleep. In *Mac-Beth*, I think. I think about it when I lie in bed. Sleep's like a balm, one I can't seem to achieve, uh, which I can't get. (*Nervous.*) Do I sound a little crazy? Never mind — I think all of us are a little. That's probably what makes us all interesting and different. People are interesting. If they'd only let themselves be different . . . That contradicts what I said before, doesn't it, about people I mean?

(4) COR: Uh —

(5) CEE: Never mind. I need to talk.

What the reader should particularly note here is that the counselee uses words like a verbal smoke screen. She hides behind them and keeps the counselor at a distance with them. This may be a function of the fear and anxiety she feels because this is a first interview; or it may be her method of relating to new people. No matter. Notice the counselor's first (1) statement contained the word "alone," which precipitated a long, involved, somewhat disjointed verbal Niagara. This word evidently has very strong meaning for the counselee. Quite obviously, there is considerable subjective and indigenous emotion attached to it. This occurs again in response to the counselor's use of the word "dorm" in the third (3) statement he makes. The counselor's second statement (2), an attempt at both clarifying and reflecting counselee feeling, is appropriate and done well, as is evidenced by the counselee's reaction (3): "Exactly." And, of course, to be sensitive not only to the words, but also to the feeling tones attached to the words, is the function of the counselor here.

Behavioral

McNair, Lorr, and Callahan (1963) have found that words are not the sole means of communication in counseling. Some counselees use facial expression denoting fear and rage (Thompson and Meltzer, 1964), while other counselees attempt to relate via physical symptoms (Bixenstine and Page, 1964). Other examples of behavioral communication include grimaces, crying, laughing, hand and arm waving. Very often this mode of communication is merely a product of the counselee's blocked emotion, blocked feeling. Conversely, and ironically enough, the counselee will react in a behavioral way because of the friendly, warm climate which the counselor has helped to create. Thus, it is not at all uncommon for a friendly, accepting counselor to find himself at the initial interview with a client who suddenly bursts into tears. The tears, in such a case, may very well be a compliment to the counselor's ability to meet the client's needs and/or a function of the client's relief to find himself in an atmosphere of freedom. Apparently, the counselor can also utilize behavioral communication effectively. For example, Matarazzo, et al., (1964a) found that simple head-nodding by the counselor can increase a counselee's speech duration.

Now, quite probably the average counselee will use not just *one* of the above modes of communication but a combination of them. Thus, the initial counseling session for many a counselee may involve not only simple words, but also words charged with emotion. In this same session, too, the counselee may grimace, weep, wave his arms and hands, and laugh heartily.

Following is an example of the three modes of communication (simple verbal, complex verbal, and behavioral) in an initial counseling contact. The counselee is a fifteen-year-old high school girl whom the principal has just suspended for smoking. She has just come into the counseling office on her own, with no appointment.

CEE: I, I, I simply have to talk to someone. I just got thrown out of school. (*Bursts into tears.*)

COR: (*Handing her some kleenex.*) (*Quietly.*) I'm sorry. Tell me about it.

CEE: (*Still weeping softly.*) There isn't much to tell really. I was in the girls' room, and the study hall teacher, Miss Jones, followed me, I guess, and surprised me when I was lighting a cigarette. And now I'm out for a whole week.

COR: I see.

[PAUSE]

What upset you most about all this — (*trailing off deliberately*).

CEE: God. I can imagine what my father's going to say!

COR: Your father's going to be upset.

CEE: He'll kill me. He'll kill me. I know. He really will.

COR: He'll be very upset.

CEE: He'll be furious. There'll be all kinds of punishments, I'm sure. I won't be able to go out for a while, for a long while probably.

COR: I see.

CEE: That's not what bothers. What bothers me is what'll happen when he finds out. How will I ever tell him. Oh, God! (*Starts weeping again.*)

Quite obviously, the printed word is not the best way to convey to the reader either the client's anxiety and anguish, or the meaning which words and physical behavior can have *to* the counselor. However, the above client's tears and her words — "I've just got to talk to someone. God, I can imagine what my father's going to say! He'll kill me. Oh, God!" — are sufficiently charged emotionally to suggest that communication here was on all levels: verbally simple, verbally complex, and behavioral.

In summary, if the initial counseling session is to be a successful one, there must be communication between the participants. The counselee, by his mere presence, and particularly if he has referred himself, seeks to communicate and to get near to the counselor. The counselor's dynamics must be of a nature not only to permit, but also to facilitate and to promote, interchanges which are verbally simple, verbally complex, and behavioral. Quite probably, the counselor who can do this will have productive and rewarding first sessions. The counselor who can not facilitate, permit, and promote communication will find only difficulty in his work.

2

The Counselor
as a Participant

Counselor Needs and Characteristics

What sort of person is the counselor? Like anybody else, he has basic needs, such as security, acceptance, self-esteem. This fact the author has treated elsewhere (Perez, 1965). But are there needs which, if not unique, at least are common to counselors? The research seems to suggest that there are. Munson (1961), for example, found that nurturance — the need to emotionally shelter and take care of people — is a major need of the counselor. Mills and Abeles (1965) found that, in addition to nurturance and affiliation, the need to like people is a major need of the counselor. Another and more recent study, however, with the same principal researcher (Mills, Chestnut, and Hartzell, 1966), has shown that the counselor seeks not so much to be nurturant as to be "warm and passionate, intuitive and psychologically penetrating."

There are indications, however, that a counselor may be understood not so much by his particular needs as by his general personality. For example, Schwebel, Karr, and Slotkin (1959) think that the essential characteristic for a counselor is "an integrated mood of relating to people. . . ." A study by Ellsworth (1963) seems to support this idea.

20

This researcher found that there was a close relationship between the counselor's ability to relate to people and his ability to relate to his client.

In addition, it would seem that the techniques the counselor employs and the effectiveness of these are basically a function of his personality. A study by Wallach and Strupp (1960) found this to be true: ". . . personality factors of the therapist are an integral part of his clinical judgments and therapeutic procedure." It has been noted, however, that, of all the techniques and procedures which the counselor must learn in order to function effectively, the most important one is that which he brings to the training situation — namely, his own style, his own personality. Williamson's (1962) observation is a good one: ". . . the style of living of the counselor himself is an extremely important and effective technique in counseling." This observation by Williamson receives some substantiation in a study by Soper and Combs (1962), who found that clients are interested in the counselor-person, not in his techniques. Most counselees are interested in the counselor who is active and reactive, a person who is a human being. Goodstein and Grigg (1959) have made this same observation: ". . . clients do not experience disembodied, theoretically-oriented counseling technique, but rather a real-life counselor who is reacting to them." A study by Pohlman (1961) strongly supports the idea that the most desirable counselor is an active, involved one. The Committee on Professional Preparation and Standards of the American Personnel and Guidance Association (1963) feels that the professionally oriented counselor is one who has "(1) belief in each individual, (2) commitment to individual human values, (3) alertness to the world, (4) open-mindedness, (5) understanding of self, and (6) professional commitment." All of these comments, studies, and observations are significant in that they throw some light on what sort of a person the counselor is, or — at least — what he is ideally.

The Counselor's View of Himself

What does the counselor think of himself and his role? An even more appropriate question for this monograph might be: How does the counselor perceive himself in the initial counseling contact?

Following is an excerpted tape of a counselor in his first meeting with a group of six college students. These students have been placed on academic probation. Part of the probation (an administrative rule of the college) involves meeting with the counselor once a week. The reader should understand, then, that each counselee below was authoritatively referred. The author finds this tape excerpt valuable in that it reflects the personality and beliefs of a very effective counselor and a genuine human being:

CEE 1: Uh, so what are we supposed to do here, huh?

COR: What would you like to do?

CEE 2: Who knows? We're here — I'm here, anyway — because Dean B. sent us.

COR: How do you feel about being here?

CEE 3: I don't know how I feel, and I won't know until you tell me, tell us, what we're supposed to do and what you're supposed to do, 'specially what you're supposed to do.

COR: What *I'm* supposed to do? (*Chuckle.*) Uh, well, I'm uh, supposed to help you all to find yourselves.

CEE 3: Find ourselves? What, are we lost?

> [LAUGHTER FROM ALL, INCLUDING THE COUNSELOR]
> [PAUSE]

CEE 4: What do you mean, "find ourselves"?

CEE 5: I know what he means. He means we're all kind of lost, like academically.

CEE 3: Is that what you mean?

COR: Yes, you're all here because you weren't doing terribly well academically —

CEE 2: Weren't doing terribly well? Christ, we flunked — almost right out of the college!

> [CHUCKLES]

CEE 1: You're going to help us try to find out why we're flunking, right?

COR: I hope so. Yes, I hope so.

CEE 3: How you going to do that, huh?

COR: Well, by talking and exploring —

CEE 3: Talking. Ha! Talking never solved nothin'!

> [PAUSE]

CEE 5: We're supposed to talk, and he's going to take apart what we say and throw it back in our faces and then make us see why we're flunking. Isn't that right?

COR: Well, you're supposed to talk, right, and I hope you'll come to see why you're flunking, yes. See, I think you can — all of you — make up your minds about things. You all can solve your own problems, whatever they may be.

CEE 3: Well, if we can solve our own problems, what are we doing here?

CEE 4: Somebody must think we can't. We got ordered here — at least I did. Ole' Pansy Puss [Dean B.] sent me, sent us all here. Did you have anything to do with that?

COR: No.

CEE 5: Do you agree with the idea of sending and ordering kids to come here? I mean, you just said —

CEE 3: Yeah, how can you force people to talk, huh?

COR: You can't. And I certainly wouldn't even attempt to try. I can't. That's not my job, and besides, I'm not even interested in trying. I'm not interested in instructing you; I'm not going to tell you what to do or how to do it; and I'm certainly not going to try to act as a disciplinarian. And in answer to your question, No, I do not agree with the idea of ordering students to come here. I do think it's a good idea to recommend to a student to come once. But I feel he should decide for himself after that. The student should decide what he wants to do after the first meeting.

[PAUSE]

CEE 2: Is anybody going to check on us whether we come or we don't come?

COR: I'm not going to check, that's for sure. (*Chuckle.*)

CEE 4: Pansy Puss'll check, don't worry!

CEE 2: Oh.

[PAUSE]

CEE 3: I don't study, that's why I'm flunking.

CEE 2: No big, dark mystery there!

CEE 1: I don't study neither.

CEE 6: Oh, this is all a lot of foolishness. We're all flunking because we're not as good as a lot of the other students. That's it. That's all of it.

CEE 3: What do you mean "we're not as good"? Speak for yourself!

CEE 2: Yeah, what are you, a psychologist or something?

CEE 6: No, I'm not a psychologist; I'm honest.

CEE 1: Uh, why, what a thing to say!

CEE 6: Uh, I'm honest.

CEE 2: Honest! You make it sound like bad manners are a requirement for honesty!

CEE 3: Never mind him. I want to, want to find out why I'm flunking.

CEE 6: Well —

CEE 6: Uh, look, why don't you just stay in the dorm and let us work on it if you're not interested? I'm interested.

CEE 2: Me, too. But I don't think I really get it, uh, what you're supposed to do, doc. Will you advise us?

COR: Well, no, because I'm not an advisor, you see. (*Chuckle.*) I can understand how it must be; how you're all sort of puzzled about what this is all about, this group counseling. No, I'm not an advisor. I don't give advice. That would mean I had all the answers. That would mean I didn't believe you could solve your own problems, all of you. I believe you can. I can't give you advice. I just don't know everything. I'm just not Baby Jesus. I don't know everything. If I did, I'd give you all the advice you could stand.

Even in print this counselor communicates his respect, tolerance, and understanding. His constant communications seem to be "I seek only to understand you," and "whatever decisions you make, I will try to understand them, too." It is this kind of a counselor whom Rogers (1961) described as "psychologically mature" because he creates "the optimal helping relationship."

The Counselor's Approach to the Initial Contact

Before a counselor can involve himself in any "optimal helping relationship," he has to have some understanding, some appreciation, of the thoughts and feelings with which he approaches the new counselee. To throw some additional light on this idea, the author asked five practicing counselors to respond to the following question: *With what thoughts, what feelings, do you approach the initial counseling contact?*

The counselors included four men and one woman. They range in age from twenty-eight to forty-five and function respectively in a college, a mental health clinic, a psychiatric hospital, and two high schools. Their resumes follow:

Counselor A — A college counselor, male

Before answering the above question, I would like to indicate that my experience to date has been in counseling situations with high school, junior college, and university students. The type of counseling I have engaged in would be classified under categories normally referred to as educational, vocational, and personal. In the last category, I have attempted to assist individuals to work through and solve personality disorders and neurotic tendencies.

I must confess that, as a full-time counselor seeing eight to ten students in forty to sixty-minute sessions, I often had little time to reflect about the initial interview.

I look upon my role or function as that of a helping or assisting individual. No doubt certain attitudes which I have, relative to human growth and development and to the causal factors of personality disorders, affect my outlook.

I normally approach the initial counseling situation with thoughts and feelings which can best be described as those of interest and concern. I entered the field of counseling because of an interest in and concern for others. As I come to understand these others, I am coming to understand myself. It is because of this that I have developed a basic feeling of confidence and trust in my ability to work with and assist students. On the other hand, I understand and am aware of my limitations. Hence, I enter the initial counseling situation with feelings of interest and concern, coupled with confidence and a desire to assist others as they strive to solve personal problems or seek greater fulfillment.

Counselor B — A counselor in a mental health clinic, male

Many ideas cross my mind as I try to organize my thoughts about the question "With what thoughts, what feelings, do you approach the initial counseling contact?" The most satisfactory approach seems to be to try and dimensionalize my feelings into several broad categories. These categories are not mutually exclusive, but serve only as illustrations of my concerns prior to an initial therapeutic contact.

The first area of concern can be grouped under the heading of "personal-emotional factors." By this, I mean my concern over the potentially emotion-arousing quality of establishing a relationship with another human being. At one level, there is the concern over just meeting a person. Even after many years of meeting people, there is still some concern at meeting someone new. On a more pertinent level, there is concern with such possibilities as: Will I like the client? Will the client like me? Does it seem as though we can establish a positively-toned working relationship? Obviously, these factors will have an influence on how effective the potential therapeutic relationship may become.

Another level concerns the type of emotional commitment or reaction the client may expect or try to arouse in me. For example, will he be depressed, angry, demanding, agitated, pleading, or distant and aloof. These reactions, in turn, will have a counter-effect on me. Can I withstand the onslaught of these feelings? Will I be astute enough to recognize them? And will I be able to use them therapeutically?

In addition, behind the manifest emotional pull of the client's symptom behavior will be the subtle, less obvious dynamic demands of the client. In a sense, the client's symptoms have an arousing quality. However, over time his long-standing interpersonal patterns of interaction will emerge, and these in turn have an emotional tinge.

The client will attempt to develop patterns of interpersonal relations that probably are part of the difficulty in his adjustment. These patterns tend to draw out emotional reactions from others. Will I, as the therapist, be able to recognize them? Should I point them out? Can I respond to them adequately? One quickly learns that you can not be all things to all people. Therefore, I feel the need to recognize as rapidly as possible what the emotional demands may be, so that if I can not use this dynamically developing relationship therapeutically, referral might be a consideration.

A second area of concern can be thought of under the heading of "intellectual-therapeutic factors." By this, I am referring to factors centering around the patient's motivation and my possible therapeutic maneuvers. Here I am focusing on such questions as: How "disturbed" is the client? Are there signs of intellectual deterioration? Is there a strong history of "acting out"? These features have implications for the type of approach one might take, the need for external contact, and the extent to which one might probe or be supportive. I am also concerned with such matters as the client's degree of psychological sophistication: Is the client oriented toward conversational therapy, or is he looking for a "magical cure-all"? Does the client seem introspective, or is he looking for immediate symptom relief with little indication of a willingness to go farther into his problems? Is the client talkative, or will he have to be prodded? What other resources has he tried before coming for psychological help? What does he hope to gain from therapy? Finally, I am concerned with sources of environmental stress that might influence the therapeutic process.

Counselor C — A counselor in a psychiatric hospital, male

Having done most of my therapy work in large federal or state institutions, I approach the initial contact in a cautious and somewhat pessimistic way. The reason for this relates directly to the referral process and the type of patient referred. All too often the patient is not self-referred, has no particular interest in a verbal form of treatment, and simply is "going along with the doctor." Many of these patients are "ward behavior problems." Others are young patients who "need something" in the way of treatment, regardless of the chronicity and severity of their individual difficulties. Occasionally, a patient agrees quite readily to participate in a treatment program with the primary objective being to get "privileges," with no real intent for treatment. Very rarely do I meet the self-referred or willing patient who is highly motivated to deal with his or her difficulty with a highly verbal "depth" therapy approach. I am aware that I am not painting a pretty picture, and I don't mean to suggest that many of these patients are not amenable to some form of therapeutic intervention; but for me this "cautious pessimism" is the most comfortable approach.

In my experience, many institutionalized patients — self-referred or otherwise — are not amenable to an "insight" type of therapy. More often than not, supportive treatment combined with a carefully thought-out "manipulation of the environment" is the preferred means. Thus, for many patients, self-referred or not, highly motivated or not, the initial contact — in an institutional environment — is primarily an attempt to assess the status of this person's life situation. It matters little, for example, that this fellow is a manipulator and thinks he can get extra privileges by coming to "class," as therapy is often called, because if I can make this appraisal, I can also control the type, length, and depth of the treatment program. Secondly, a realistic appraisal of the type, depth, and duration of the illness, as well as the individual's control abilities and ego status, is an absolute must. Again, it matters little whether this individual is chronic or acute, psychotic or anxiety-laden; what is more important is that these factors be clear in my mind so that I can think of some useful way of approaching this person. Finally, an assessment of the person's social and economic status is invaluable. It matters little that this individual is absolutely penniless; what is important is that his family is willing to give him a place to stay and some money to help him get back on his feet.

Now I'd like to get back to this attitude of "cautious pessimism." It is based on the feeling that in an institutional environment I'm going to "strike out" as often as I succeed and that very often my successes will be based on rather restricted and limited goals. What I mean by this is that combining the referral motive with psychological, social, and economic factors, as well as my personal limitations and preferences and the limitations of the institution, I come up with first a decision as to whether I can be of any value to this individual and, if so, how.

As far as I'm concerned, the eclectic approach is the one for me. I've given up being concerned with whether I have "cured the patient." As a matter of fact, I don't even know what that means. I've not had much experience with therapy outside of an institutional setting, so I can't say that my attitude of cautious pessimism would be changed or modified under other circumstances. I tend to doubt it, however.

One conclusion I have derived from my institutional experience is that some types of psychological problems are not yet clearly enough understood to be dealt with effectively. And even where they are better understood, to deal with simply the psychological aspects within the individual to the exclusion of the physical, social, and economic environment is not an effective method of treatment. Often these factors are beyond control and again the eclectic principle, as far as I'm concerned, is the best guideline.

Counselor D — A high school counselor, female

With what thoughts, what feelings, do I approach the initial counseling contact? Well, I wonder, will I be of service; will I satisfy this client's need so positively that he will leave the interview with some feeling of satisfaction? Generally, I am sure there is some slight feeling of apprehension and the feeling of anticipation is present also, for there is the experience of a new relationship. I never cease to marvel at this last feeling.

Counselor E — A high school counselor, male

After seventeen years, I still continue to wonder about my adequacy. Every session is different; every client is different. There is little significant pattern from person to person or from one initial contact to another. They are all different. This constant difference has made me very alert and — I like to think — sensitive to what the client may need from me. I suppose that's the only thing which they all have in common: they *need.*

I wonder and I worry if I can put the client at his ease and if I can provide a good climate for our interaction. You see, I am ever mindful of the boy who sat in the outer office, trembling, so my secretary said, and asked the student beside him: "I've never seen the counselor before — What's he like?"

Even though I find myself getting involved, I always wonder at this ability of mine to stand aside and be objective, intellectually objective. I have to figure what he is doing to himself, to me, to us. I'm also ever mindful of the fact that I have to let him know that I am aware when he is trying to manipulate, as sometimes he must.

An Analysis of Counselor Approaches

The above responses indicate that the counselors incorporate certain common characteristics. These are:

> Concern
> Emotional Investment
> Cognitive Detachment
> Sensitivity
> Introspection

(1) The counselor is concerned. He is interested, and he cares. His concern is only a healthy one, since in every instance it is about the client and their coming relationship, not himself alone. More particularly, he is concerned about his ability to meet the client's needs. The counselor would like to be sure that his own personality will be of a quality and strength which will provide and promote a climate in which the counselee may learn to feel secure, accepted, worthy, and free. Even more, the counselor is concerned about his ability to perceive the world of the client without interference from his own defenses and needs. And if the counselor's concern includes "some slight feeling of apprehension," the apprehension may be understood not so much as dread or foreboding as a concern to be the ideal helper which Rogers (1961) described so superbly.

(2) The counselor seeks to emotionally invest in the relationship. This means that he is interested, cares, and wants only to help. The focal point of his interest is the needs of the counselee. He is interested in promoting a healthier and more balanced need satisfaction in the

counselee so that the latter can cope more effectively with the reality of his environment. He cares very much what kind of a world his client perceives, and wants to understand, appreciate, and even share that perception during the counseling hour. The counselor's rewards, both professional and personal, are derived from this investment. It is this kind of reward which leads the counselor to be "sensitive to what the client may need from me" and to observe that "I suppose that's the only thing they all have in common: they need."

(3) Despite his emotional investment, the counselor is also cognitively detached. This detachment serves important purposes. It permits him to understand the various meanings of the counselee's words, to choose his own words more appropriately, and to utilize the various counseling techniques available to him as effectively as possible. In addition, cognitive or intellectual detachment permits the counselor not only to maintain some measure of perspective about the counseling relationship, but — even more important — it allows him to evaluate his worth to the counselee. But most important is the fact that cognitive detachment helps the counselor to maintain his separateness from the counselee, his identity as a counselor. His needs, his feelings, his perception, and his interactive style — all the dynamics which make up his personality — continue to be peculiarly his *only* if he is able to maintain his cognitive detachment. Very important, too, such detachment will prevent the counselor from being overwhelmed by the feelings, behaviors, and general demands of the counselee; or, to paraphrase one of the above counselors, cognitive detachment helps the counselor to "withstand the onslaught of client feelings and be astute enough to recognize and to use them therapeutically." Such detachment by the counselor, then, has an additional merit: it permits the counselee to retain *his* integrity, his needs, his feelings, his perceptions, and his interactive style. Only by permitting the counselee this integrity can the counselor help the counselee to a greater emotional maturity.

(4) The counselor is a sensitive person. He is aware of the subtlety of communicative modes. He is equally tuned to the fact that the counselee "needs" and that his most fundamental need is to be understood both in feeling and in thought. His sensitivity extends to the ability to tolerantly insinuate himself (and communicate the fact) into the client's world, to perceive the world as the client does, and to appreciate the rationale for the client's interactive style and his meaning derivatives.

(5) The counselor is introspective. He is a soul-searcher. He questions himself, his motives, and his feelings. This is done not out of any unhealthy neurotic need, but only to understand himself and the reality

in which he is steeped. His self-perception is accurate, healthy, and conducive to an understanding of his own needs and defenses and of how they influence his counseling. This self-perception has also led to an understanding and appreciation of his limitations as a counselor. It is this penchant for introspection which leads him to make observations such as: "I have developed a basic feeling and trust in my ability to work with and assist many students."

The Creative Counselor

A study by Carkhuff and Truax (1965) indicates that a mere hundred hours of training may be enough for some people to function effectively as therapists. Wrenn (1960) found that theoretical orientation — i.e., non-directive, analytic — does not determine how effective the counselor is in his response to the client. And again, Strupp (1957) compared a non-directivist (Rogers) with a psychoanalyst (Wolberg) and found that both were "warm, accepting, and non-critical; both encouraged the patient's expression of feelings; and . . . greater self-acceptance in their patients." What all these studies show is that experience, theoretical orientation, and technique acquiring are not the critical determinants for effective counseling. Strongly implied in these studies is that the effective counselor can be measured more easily and more accurately by his personal qualities than by the nature of his education and training.

What is an effective counselor? An effective counselor is a creative counselor. And what is a creative counselor? The creative counselor incorporates certain qualities. These are:

1. Intelligence
2. Security
3. Authenticity
4. Motivation
5. The capacity to derive meaning from
   each counseling experience.

(1) The creative counselor is cognitively intelligent. This does not mean that he has to function with an IQ of over 140 to be effective. On the other hand, the thought here is that there need not be any upper limits to his capacity — only lower limits. An individual who scores over 140 on a standardized intelligence test would not be hampered by such intellectual powers. But if he scored below 90, he would, in all likelihood, have difficulties as a counselor (probably because of the self-esteem problem which he would have acquired in the academic

setting). Equally important, the creative counselor is one who is *emotionally* intelligent. Emotional intelligence refers to the counselor's capacity to be not only tuned and receptive to the dynamics of his client, but — even more — to communicate an exquisite understanding of those dynamics.

(2) The creative counselor is secure. He is secure enough to participate emotionally and enjoy the counseling experience. He is secure enough to enter and involve himself in the emotional world of his client. His security is best reflected in the fact that he is not threatened by the many and varied dynamics to which he is constantly exposed. And this exposure engenders emotional involvement which, in turn, means that often he permits the client to take a look into his (the counselor's) dynamics.

(3) The creative counselor is honest. He is an authentic human being. As Burton (1964) has observed: "Psychotherapy is helpful when it is given by an authentic person. . . ." The overt behavior, the language, the commitment to his client and to his profession are expressed cognitively, but they are based on emotional conviction. When, as noted in (2) above, a client takes a look into the counselor's emotional life, he finds a human being who is sincere in his honesty, in his authenticity. The cognitive level reflects the emotional level truly. Shoben (1962) expressed these thoughts well when he wrote that "the counselor who achieves this kind of honesty in dealing with his cognitive self is likely to enjoy a sense of personal growth in his professional life that is denied to others." Such a counselor's communication system (verbal, simple, complex, and behavioral) is consistent. In counseling at least, the counselor says, feels, and does only what he means.

(4) The creative counselor is motivated. He is motivated not only to emotionally invest in his clients, but to innovate his mode for professional involvement. He can do this because, as we have noted, he is both secure and authentic. His constant motivation is to become his potential, not only as a counselor but — more important — as a human being in his total life. Even more, the motivated counselor is a searcher. His search necessarily involves change. Note that the counselor is not threatened by change either in the client or in himself. On the contrary, he is quite receptive to it and is changing constantly. This change may be more accurately understood as a constant growth — personal and professional. This growth is in the direction of self-fulfillment or what Maslow has termed "self-actualization."

(5) Finally, the creative counselor is one who can derive meanings from each counseling experience. In this regard, Osgood and Suci

(1957) have observed that ". . . the significance of meaning as a most critical variable in personality is most apparent perhaps in the process of therapy itself. . . ." The meanings derived from the counseling interaction are both cognitive and emotional and serve as the catalysts for his constant professional growth. These meanings also serve to clarify his thoughts about his work and provide him with the emotional strength to withstand failure and professional criticisms.

3

The Counselee
as a Participant

What does the research show about the counselee's personality? There is evidence which indicates that the counselee has emotional and intellectual traits which set him apart from the individual who does not seek counseling. For example, Mendelsohn and Kirk (1962) have found that, compared with non-counselees, counselees are less judgmental and feeling, but more intuitive and introverted. Kirk (1955) found that the counselee is often of a very high scholastic calibre. This researcher discovered that 28 percent of the students in Phi Beta Kappa sought counseling, while only 22 percent from the general student body did so.

Equally important, there is evidence to indicate that the counselee's personality is going to determine how effective the counselor's particular approach will be (Sonne and Goldman, 1957). This study seems to find support in a study conducted by Strickland and Crowne (1963), who found that a counselee's motivations influence the counselor's perception and, we can infer, the subsequent interaction.

Understandably enough, what transpires in the counseling hour is determined in large measure by the counselee's personality (Phillips, Matarazzo, Matarazzo, Saslow, and Kanfer, 1961). Phillips, et al., found that the counselee who is "oriented towards other people speaks less often, responds quickly, and is more dominant in the interview." The client who is not inclined toward interaction is one who "loses or submits to interruption, is hesitant in speaking, and is less active verbally."

The Problem of Anxiety

The most common characteristic of the individual who seeks counseling probably is the all-pervasive, debilitating nature of his anxiety. This anxiety can take varied forms. Some of these forms are as follows:

(1) Anxiety can be quite diffused and specific to no object, place, or person. The individual may find he has no defense with which to control his worries. Quite probably, he doesn't even know what he's worried about. All he knows is that he labors under constant tensions which will not abate.

(2) The anxiety may also be expressed in such states as sleepwalking, amnesia, sudden and uncontrollable desires to flee, or insomnia.

(3) The anxiety may be phobic in character; i.e., contact with dirt, high places, policeman, etc., may precipitate uncontrollable or paralyzing anxiety.

(4) The anxiety may show itself in an hypochondriacal way. The counselee may come to counseling with an unusual number of aches, pains, and general somatic problems for which no physical cause exists.

What the counselor should understand also is that one of the reasons the counselee is beset by this debilitating anxiety is that his psychological defenses (i.e., denial, rationalization, fantasy, compensation, intellectualization) are not working effectively. Very often this ineffectiveness of defenses works to cripple his perception of reality. He may see poorly, hear incorrectly, or — even worse — his reactions to others may be inappropriate. His moods may vary tremendously, and very often he has little understanding and appreciation of his feelings.

Quite understandably, with such inaccurate or distorted perceptions, his interactions are unrewarding. People generally do not find him attractive because he does not see, hear, or react to them appropriately. In other words, he has trouble communicating with others because his cues to others are vague; and in addition, he is unable to effectively read the cues of others.

The thought here, then, is that the counselee is one who has difficulty binding or controlling anxiety. Furthermore, it is crucial for a counselor to understand the nature of his client's anxiety and — more important still — the conflicts which precipitate that anxiety. Quite simply, the counselee is a conflicted person (except possibly the individual who is authoritatively referred), and one who experiences considerable difficulty in binding the anxiety resulting from that conflict. More often than not, the conflict deals, on the one hand, with the healthy desire to change a neurotic pattern of behavior and, on the other, with the fear of change. Very probably, the fear of changing one's behavior is the reason why so many counselees persevere in a neurotic way, i.e., in a way that is self-destructive and/or destructive toward others. For many a counselee, the neurotic way is, if not the most comfortable way, at least the most familiar way.

Thus, for many counselees entry into counseling is not so much a search for behavior change as it is an attempt to have their anxiety reduced. Weitz (1961), for example, has noted that "the expectation of anxiety reduction by the intervention of the counselor" is a common characteristic of most counseling interviews.

Also, the counselor should know that the counselee's general level of anxiety invariably is at peak level during the initial interview. There are several reasons for this: the unique nature of the experience, differences between counselor and client attitudes toward counseling (Van der Veen and Stoler, 1965), and differences between counselor and client in expectation of roles (Kanfer, 1965; Clemes and D'Andrea, 1965).

Not uncommonly, these differences give rise to feelings of guilt and thinking along such lines as "I don't think the way the counselor does. What's the matter with me? There must be something the matter with me." Such thoughts, of course, reinforce existing low feelings of self-esteem.

For some counselees these differences give vent to feelings of resentment. This is particularly true of that counselee who views the world in a narrow, rigid way. His basic, emotional position is that a person — any person — should perceive the world *his* way. He is strongly resentful of those who do not agree with him, and is often surprised if people do. What this type of counselee perceives, then, is a hostile, threatening world where people are more inclined to hate and harm him than to love and help him. Of course, with such a perception of the world, he usually finds that people are not so much loving as unkind; thereby he confirms his original perception, which is what he sought to do in the first place! What is being described here, of course, is a suspicious individual. Suspicious people ordinarily have very intricate defense systems — denial supported by projection, rationalization, and displacement of hostility.

With respect to this last, the author's experience has been that more and more the displacement defense is becoming an archaic and inadequate defense for the middle-class counselee. Not uncommonly, it is this knowledge ("I can't vent my hostility with fits or fists!") which raises the client's anxiety and sends him into counseling.

Often the counselee harbors strong feelings of helplessness. He is confused, bewildered, and shaken. A familiar defense mode, for no reason apparent to him, proves inadequate in meeting his needs. The counselee does not know what to do. It is precisely at this time — when he is in a period of emotional turmoil between discarding and retaining an inadequate defense, an inaccurate perception, or an ineffective way of interacting — that the counselee comes into counseling.

Arbuckle (1961) has observed that the counselee's personality is generally characterized by low self-esteem. This observation is supported in a study by Hollon and Zolik (1962), who found also that the counselor who is successful in meeting this particular need of the client will meet with professional success.

In brief, then, the research and current thought seem to indicate that at the initial interview the counselor can expect to meet a client who is laboring under an all-pervasive anxiety. Associated with this anxiety are certain other potentially destructive feelings or attitudes. These are:

1. Fear
2. Guilt
3. Resentment
4. Suspiciousness
5. Helplessness
6. Low self-esteem

All of the above-mentioned may contribute significantly to the complexity of the client's problems, increase his high anxiety, and consequently, may be a severe hindrance to effective interpersonal relationships.

The following excerpt from an initial interview illustrates most of these feelings. The client is a seventeen-year-old boy. The setting is a high school counseling office.

Cor: So, your feelings are that Mr. A. doesn't like you?

Cee: Doesn't like me! That's putting it mildly. He can't stand me. He can't stand having me in his gym class or on any athletic teams, either. And I don't know why, either. I suppose it's some sort of a personality clash or something like that. And I'll say this, too — he never gave me a break right from the start. Right from the start he had it in for me. I remember when he came up to the junior high school when I was in the eighth grade. I was always good in basketball. The day he came to watch I was playing on the ninth grade team. I was that good. Well, it was hot that day and I sank five foul shots and made eleven baskets. Twenty-seven points I made!!* Nobody'd ever

---

* In a subsequent interview, the client admitted he had never scored more than ten or eleven points in a game.

done *that* before — nobody! 'Least not while I was there. And you know what he said after the game? You know what he said? "Think you're pretty good, huh?" Instead of saying "Gee, that was pretty good, kid;" instead of slapping me on the back, he says in that sneering way he's got: "Think you're pretty good, huh?" Now what the hell kind of way is that to do? There I was a little eighth-grader. We all knew he was coming down that day. We were all nervous, waiting that day. I mean, to us it was like God or something coming. I mean, the coach of the high school! A guy who won nine city championships in basketball, coming to scout *us!* I mean, geez! So then what's he say to me? "Think you're pretty good, huh?"

[PAUSE]

COR: That statement made a very lasting impression.

CEE: What?

COR: I say, that statement of his, "Think you're pretty good, huh?" made a strong impression on you —. You've remembered it over four years.

CEE: Well, I don't know if it did or not. He just never gave me a break. Right from the start. So screw him! Who needs him!

COR: You feel that right from the start he never gave you a break.

CEE: Right. Right from the start. I got to this school as a sophomore. He'd heard of me. He knew me. When I was in ninth grade, I broke every record they had in the junior high. You can't tell me he never heard of me. I'm not trying to brag or anything; but I did — I broke all the records. So what are you supposed to do? So what more can I do?

COR: That sort of thing makes you feel, uh, like there's not much point in doing your best, uh, in performing well, because it doesn't seem to be appreciated.

CEE: Right.

COR: It kind of makes you feel helpless.

CEE: Yeah.

[SILENCE]

COR: You do your best and —

CEE: Right. I did my best, and I did a lot, too. I broke every damned record, and it wasn't enough. I mean, what's the matter with me? I mean, the whole thing sort of gives you the creeping willies. I mean, did I do something wrong? I mean, if I did, I didn't do it on purpose or anything. I mean, for God's sake!

COR: If you offended him, you don't know how.

CEE: Yeah.

[SILENCE]

COR: Or at least if you did, you did not do it on purpose.

CEE: Right. And even if I did, he didn't have to hold it against me for my whole high school life. I mean, Christ! Enough's enough — if you know what I mean.

COR: You think the punishment's far exceeded any crime you might have committed.

CEE: Damn right. I don't know what I did, but whatever I did, I don't deserve what I got for treatment here. I mean, he never let me play ball for one reason or another. I mean, like the first year he caught me smoking and bounced me off the junior varsity team for the whole year. He never did that before.* He hasn't done it since, neither. The second year he played me only two times in the whole year. So I quit before the last game. He never even came to ask me about it. I mean, so what the heck's he got it in for me for? I mean, oh, so I don't know. I never did anything.

COR: You feel that his treatment of you has been most unfair. He never treated you fairly when you were on the basketball team. As far as you know, you're the only one whom he's ever bounced off the junior varsity. You've never done anything to hurt him.

CEE: How can I hurt him? I mean, well once I said something about his wife — maybe I shouldn't have said.

COR: You said something about his wife?

CEE: Yeah, maybe I shouldn't have said that. I didn't mean it. I've felt bad about it ever since.

[SILENCE]

COR: You've felt bad.

CEE: Yeah.

COR: Sort of guilty like.

CEE: (*Sigh.*) Yeah.
(*Pause.*) (*Expelling his breath loudly.*) Christ, I wish I'd never seen his wife. Funny part about the whole business is that I haven't seen her since and I never saw her before that day. Christ, what could I do?

[SILENCE]

COR: I see. And you figure that what you said has been bothering Mr. A. all these years.

CEE: Yeah.

[SILENCE]

COR: I see.

CEE: See, what I said was not very nice. In fact, you might say it was pretty bad.

COR: Hm-m-m-m.

CEE: See, I was with a bunch of guys. It was when I was in the ninth grade, and he came to see the crop of guys that was going up to the high school the following year. And it wasn't all my fault really, 'cause I remembered how he hadn't even given me a little compliment on the way I'd played the year before when I got twenty-seven points. So I was teed off at him. So anyway, I was sitting on the bench just before the game when he came up with his wife; and I remember looking across the gym floor — see, they had to walk by us and across the floor to get to the bleachers — and I remember sort of looking over Mrs. A, and I said when they were only about, I don't know, ten

---

* In truth, Mr. A. had suspended dozens of players over the years.

feet away from us, I said: "Christ, is she a beast!" That's what I said and I've been sorry ever since. Can you imagine anyone being that stupid? That's me. Sometimes I think I deserved what I got from him. (*Loud expulsion of breath.*)

Cor: Mr. A. heard you.

Cee: Oh, he heard me. Don't you worry about that! He heard me alright. She didn't turn around, but *he* did.

[Pause]

And he looked right at me. He knew it was me. He knew who said the words. In fact, I thought for a second he was going to say something. His mouth sort of worked up and down, but no words came out. And then he turned around and went with his wife.

[Pause]

I guess I played about the worst game of my life that night. I made only two baskets. I fouled out of the game at the end of the third quarter. I hogged the ball. I was lousy. When the chips are down, I'm always lousy. That's me. That's the real me. I know that's what a lot of the guys say. Sometimes I think that maybe he never gave me a break because he thinks I'm a lousy player because of that night. But I think, I think that's 'cause I don't want to think that he's holding a grudge against me, 'cause of what I said about his wife. If you know what I mean.

Cor: (*Clearing his throat*) Yeah, I know what you mean. You don't like to think that he dislikes you because of a mistake you made a long time ago as a kid. You regret that mistake and wish that he judged you on your ability as an athlete.

Cee: You got it. I mean, Christ, what can I do about it? It's done. It's over. It's been done and over for four years. What can I do? All I want to do is forget it.

Cor: Yes, I see. You wish he'd forget it.

Cee: Yeah.

Cor: All you want to do is forget it.

Cee: Yeah.

Cor: There's nothing you can do.

Cee: Yeah.

[Silence]

I thought of going to him and apologizing. But it's not the kind of thing you can do easy or even at all, if you know what I mean. The next time I even saw him was six months after I said it. I knew he didn't forget it. The look he gave me made me want to die. But I couldn't bring myself to go and say "I'm sorry, coach, about what I said about your wife!" It would've seemed like, I don't know, like "I hurt you, and now I want you to forget it and treat me right." Somehow it never seemed right.

[Pause]

Cor: You figure you should have been punished for what you said about Mrs. A.

Cee: Yeah, I do.

[Pause]

Boy, I worried about it the whole summer before I got here from junior high. I knew he was going to hold it against me. Mr. A.'s got a way of scaring you. He's a pretty tough guy.

The seven feelings listed just prior to the above example often effect certain weaknesses in client expression and mode of relating.

The client's obvious feelings of low self-esteem result in considerable boasting: "I was *that* good," "I made twenty-seven points." He laments, "When the chips are down, I'm always lousy. That's me."

The counselee's anxiety, fear, and suspiciousness permeate the whole interview and are reflected particularly in the client's inability to explain his problem in a short, concise way. He takes a while to get to the point. Consider, for example, the marked shift from "I don't know why Mr. A. doesn't like me," to "Christ, is she a beast! That's what I said, and I've been sorry ever since." The occasional ruminations and the loud breath expulsion often are signs of his generalized anxiety.

Feelings of guilt and helplessness seem to effect silences. The reader will note that the silences usually occur after admissions of guilt feelings or feelings of helplessness; for example: "I mean, Christ, what can I do about it? I shouldn't have said that. I didn't mean it. Christ, what can I do?"

The feelings of resentment often precipitate exaggerations and inaccuracies: "I sank five foul shots and I made eleven baskets" and "He caught me smoking and bounced me off the junior varisity — He never did that before." The prospective counselor should know that inaccuracies and exaggerations do not often come singly. Be suspect of others.

Counselee Motives and Expectations

The author felt that the reader might find it profitable to view the counseling process through the eyes of the counselees. More particularly, why does he seek counseling? What does he expect to get out of it? The counselor asked five counselees these very questions. Their replies follow:

Counselee A — a twenty-one-year-old married college senior, male, who referred himself for counseling.

There are many reasons why I have sought counseling. Probably the primary and most obvious reason is involved with my hopes of resolving the anxiety which is producing problems within me. I have sought counseling with the hope that I could better understand myself and hence those problems which affect me. My security, my way of life, was — and probably still is — threatened by the particular problem with which I was confronted.* At times, the anxiety is so bad that I want to vomit, but I can't; it continues to twist, turn, and tear at my insides. How do I deal with this? I try to be as rational as I can. In terms of being rational, I attempt to evaluate the problem itself, then myself, after which I try to understand the feelings of others involved and how they perceive the problem. I seek counseling so that I may learn more about myself, people, and how to deal with problems for the betterment of all involved.

I hope to perceive this particular problem and future problems with better understanding. If I am capable of achieving some success in this area, then maybe I'll be able to help others in their quest to understand life, its trials and tribulations.

Counselee B — a twenty-six-year-old unmarried female who has applied for help in a community mental health clinic.

I thought I was pregnant. For three months I thought I was pregnant. I left home and moved out to another state to spare my parents the shame of living with me. I'm back home now and have been home for two weeks. Even now, I don't know how to express it except to say that I went to two doctors and was told by both that I am *not* pregnant, nor was I ever pregnant, unless I miscarried — which they seem to think was highly unlikely. That's one reason I seek counseling.

Needless to say, since then I've been very shocked and confused and a good deal resentful for all the horrible pain I caused and for trusting friendships of too many people, hoping to find an answer to what was never a problem. I'm very dependent, doctor; that's why I seek counseling.

It was difficult for me to accept what the doctors said because I somehow had all the symptoms and a rabbit test to confirm my doubts; but the doctor said that tests are not infallible and that due to the test and my guilt feelings I must have had what he termed a "false" or "hysterical" pregnancy. That's another reason for my seeking counseling, doctor: I'm always feeling so guilty.

It's difficult to believe that I could have let myself carry that so far and more difficult yet to face the fact that I handled the whole thing so heinously. I involved — either directly or indirectly — so many people! The few people that I told were involved and hurt, almost as deeply, if not more so, than I; and if they weren't hurt, they were

---

* Divorce.

certainly disappointed. And the ones that just heard rumors, and there seems to be an astronomical number of those, are confused and embarrassed upon seeing me.

All the talk does not really bother me at times, and yet at other times it haunts me. It seems that I am just as guilty of a crime I didn't commit as one I might have and thought I did — that crime being that I was pregnant in society's eyes. I can see all their reasoning, but can't keep from damning it. It seems such a crime to be pregnant! Yet if I were to tell people simply that I had had intercourse and felt guilty about it, I would never have been the cause of so much talk.

But all the "if's" in the world won't bring back the past. Why do I seek counseling? I want to know what I should have known then. I want to gain from my counseling, perhaps, what I should have learned from my experience. Right now I don't know what I have learned. I think that there is a lot of invaluable knowledge in my experience. Unfortunately, I don't know how to apply it. Help me.

What do I hope to get out of it? Maybe to be wise, smart, and maybe know how I expect to be able to use what I live — if you know what I mean. Right now my impression is "I don't use what I live."

Counselee C — a twenty-year-old female, an unmarried college sopho-more, who was authoritatively referred.

Actually, I didn't seek counseling; the Dean of Women "strongly suggested" that I spend an hour a week with some member of the Psychology Department because my "internal conflicts" and "complete change of attitude" upset her. I jumped at the chance. I would have sought counseling on my own but always felt that I would be wasting the counselor's time. Talking makes me feel better, especially talking to someone who can understand what I am trying to say. A counselor is not involved in the personal life of the counselee. That means that I am free to say what I feel without having to worry about hurting anybody. Conversations are not repeated; this is very relaxing.

A lot of times counselors can point out peculiarities in your speech and thought or faults in your personality that people close to you are incapable of seeing. Also, the more you take something apart, examine it, and put it back together, the more you know about it, and yourself. This, I guess, is the basic idea that draws me to counseling. I try to talk with my friends, but they are shocked when I start to tell them how I feel about anything. They either think the whole conversation is a joke or ignore it completely. If I tell them how I feel and they understand part of it, they don't get the main point sometimes and leave with a warped, distorted picture of me. This bothers me very much. Counseling is reassuring: It gives me more confidence in myself and often gives me another view of the situation. I guess this is what I most enjoy about it and expect from it — talking to someone more capable of understanding you in a relaxed atmosphere.

Counselee D — a nineteen-year-old male college sophomore, who was referred by a member of the college faculty.

Why did I seek counseling? Well, I was told by a psych professor that perhaps counseling would solve some of my problems. I have many problems that I feel are evident to me only if I stop and think "What are my problems?" or if I happen to be involved in an argument about one of these problems — religion, parents, etc.

I have difficulty transferring my thoughts onto paper, especially in sociology — a subject which I am very interested in, yet one in which I am getting low marks on quizzes because of this difficulty. Mr. C. suggested that if I did discuss my problems with him, perhaps it would help me to see that these problems are contributing to this difficulty even though I feel that they are not.

I am a psychology major. This, I feel, has led me to seek counseling because I have read about and seen what counseling can do for an individual. I am sure that if these underlying factors are making things difficult for me, they will be made evident to me through counseling.

Another reason for my seeking assistance is because during these sessions I am talking only of my problems to an experienced person. I might be able to help myself if I had time to sit down and think my difficulties out — weigh the issues, that is, "Is this parental problem affecting my everyday life?" But my days are so tight, and being married with a daughter, working, and going to school do not afford me the time.

Also, I plan to enter the field of psychology, and how can I attempt to understand other people and solve — or attempt to solve — their problems when I cannot help myself?

Actually, all signs do point to the fact that I must need assistance in some way. A person who has experienced the problems that I have cannot possibly (although he is sure he can) pass them off and expect to go his own way without these things affecting him.

Counselee E — a nineteen-year-old college sophomore, female, who was self-referred.

Why do I seek counseling? What do I expect to get out of it? These really are not easy questions to answer.

I find myself trying very hard to study, yet my work seems to take me three times as long to complete as does my roommates', and I never seem to finish. My marks are all going down because I am not really learning. Still I am working hard, and I am always tired. In my room I am usually the last one to bed and the first up in the morning.

In classes I feel incompetent. I am afraid to participate because I might give an incorrect response and suffer the embarrassment of seeming "stupid." My fears always seem to be proven, for when I *do* speak in class discussion I am usually wrong. I either can not remember the material or think of it after the teacher has asked someone else, or I give such an incoherent answer that the teacher can not understand me. I find it hard to communicate. It bothers me to think that I am planning to be a teacher when I don't even know how to express myself. What will happen when I encounter the classroom situation?

For the most part, my teachers do not seem to be the problem. All seem to be quite helpful. One teacher I find different, however. I am critical of his approach to the subject. Being a future teacher, I guess I probably am too critical. After class I ask him to slow down and to explain a topic in a different way. I have to learn that he is the teacher and that he has his own method of teaching. I cannot change him, so I have to bend.

My school work is not all that is bothering me. I consider myself a nineteen-year-old wallflower. During high school I dated rarely. When I did go out I felt overly self-conscious. Actually I was friendly with many boys of my age. The fact was that they would all come to me with their problems. I was a good listener but very rarely was any real help. They may have treated me like a sister, but I usually ended up with a big crush on the current fellow. This continued on through high school, and I was determined not to let it happen in college. It inevitably did, however, and what dates I had seemed to be limited to the "blind dates" my friends would "fix up" for me.

Through high school I was in many major activities, held the office of president of one club and treasurer of another. I was an honor student and was liked by my teachers. My classmates respected me as someone who would get things done, but not as a member of their "cliques" or as a friend to have fun with. In college I found great improvement. There were many friends.

One of my roommates was really popular. She did well in everything and was attractive as well. I guess she was my idol. All I wanted from her was her friendship. She seemed only too willing to do things with me, but only when it would benefit her. I was doing all I could for her and getting hurt at the same time. One thing I noticed about her was that she would seem to lead fellows on and then forget about them. She probably was not conscious of the fact. I began to like a guy we both knew. Things seemed promising. Then my roommate began liking our mutual friend. I was very upset and thought she was trying to take my only hope. We would not say much to each other, we were no longer seen together, and it got to the point where I was so irritated that I could not even study in the same room with her. I came to consider her and her friends as the type who enjoyed making jokes of other people's actions. I had always thought it was a great sin to laugh at anyone; and then it was me they were laughing at — that was worst of all. I had realized that choosing her as a roommate was a big mistake. I had wanted to stay with the roommate I had the previous year, but to please those friends my former roommate and I had each consented to become the third roommate in other rooms.

I am a suitcase student in college. My parents want me home on weekends. I do the household chores that I should rightfully help out with, but I can't help but believe that I should be at school. Since Saturday is my mother's busiest work day, I help out at home. There is the cleaning to be done, and my five-year-old sister to be taken care of. My thirteen-year-old brother is a help, but I am afraid that he will become sissified if allowed to do too much "women's work." My father also can't get used to the fact that his little daughter is living away from home. I am growing up, but my parents haven't realized this. During high school I was at home most of the time; but I thought college would be different. How can I become accustomed to college life if I must go home every weekend? How can I teach youngsters responsibility when I hardly know what independence is?

And so I am confronted with all these little irritations: parents, roommates, dating, and studies. I have begun to show nervousness, irritability, and sensitivity. One day in my General Psychology class, the teacher discussed the Freudian concept of the id, the ego, and the superego. I did not understand everything he said; but as I recall it, he explained that our id harbors all our inner repressions, and they are kept there by our superego — our conscience. When many repressions are stored up, our id is working against the superego, and the signs of it are worry, tension, anxiety, etc. He further explained that the psychoanalyst attempts to reveal the causes of these frustrations; he sort of brings these problems to the surface. All of a sudden, all my worries ran through my mind at once. I could not concentrate on the lesson any longer. My eyes were filled with tears. I looked down to my notebook and took frantic notes so no one would see me cry. It was then I decided that the counseling service might do me some good. Immediately after class I asked for help.

I think that by going to a counselor maybe he will be able to listen to my troubles with an unbiased ear; and I hope he will be able to see things — the little things that are bothering me — in the proper perspective, because I can not. I feel that by talking to him I will be relieved. I have read somewhere that a psychologist sort of collects his clients' disorganized problems and puts them in logical order. Maybe if I know the real problem I can direct my efforts in dealing with it properly. Next, I could eventually perhaps become a real student, one for whom a reading assignment is just a first step — not a never-ending chore. Then perhaps I may get more out of college life. My primary reason for going to a counselor is to talk to someone.

Analysis of the Responses

It should be noticed that there are a number of common characteristics among the above responses:

(1) The counselee suffers from vague, ill-defined but very real, tensions and anxieties. The anxieties are so intense that he "wants to vomit." It is this intense anxiety which motivates the counselee to seek counseling. The counselee seems to feel that if he can learn to more effectively meet his needs of security and acceptance, his anxieties may abate. The counselee feels that his generalized anxiety interferes with his ability to cope effectively with his environment. Therefore, he does not know how to cope effectively with the threats which he encounters in his daily environment. The reader should understand that it does not matter if these dangers are fancied or real. The anxieties which these threats produce are quite real. This is all the counselee understands.

It often takes the counselee a long time to seek counseling because at one time the anxiety served a very important purpose quite effectively, namely, to alert the counselee to the dangers in his environment. But now the anxiety has extended beyond that function of alerting the individual to dangers, since it now reproduces itself. It is this latter effect which alarms him, because it is this effect which communicates to him the breakdown of his defense system. Often, it is at this point that the individual seeks counseling because his defenses serve two purposes: (1) to defend him from the actual or perceived threat in his environment and (2) to satisfy the basic psychological needs, in this case, security and acceptance.

(2) The counselee seeks to be independent, to be self-reliant. The counselor should view the counselee's apparent desire for someone to lean on as a very transitory need. To constantly nurture the need (the more sophisticated in the profession call it "supportive therapy") is to assist and abet in the growth of the passive, dependent qualities which are the foundation of much of the counselee's difficulties. Supportive therapy meets counselor needs very well; it is highly doubtful, however, that it meets those of the counselee. Its long-term effect is to produce a dependent, unresourceful individual whose direction is counselor-determined. The strong conviction here is that every client has the potential to solve his own problems, and, therefore, every client

seeks to be not dependent but resourceful; every client seeks not to be a slave but rather the entrepreneur of his feelings, emotions, and directions.

The counselee's search for independence, then, may be better understood as a search for self-esteem. Quite simply, the counselee seeks to feel worthy and — more important — to realize his best potential not only as a counselee but also as a human being. The counselee's search for self-esteem essentially is a search for confidence, the confidence to express in a socially acceptable way his own particular brand of humanity and to contribute to the society which produced and nurtures him.

(3) The counselee seeks to acquire self-knowledge and understanding. He seeks to know about himself; his needs, defenses, perception, and interactive mode. He wants to understand what dynamic rationale, if any, impels him to act in the manner he finds disturbing. Even more, he seeks to understand not only himself, but others also.

(4) The counselee seeks to relearn a new and more effective perception of the world in general, and of his reality in particular. He is concerned about his penchant to perceive hostility and threat rather than love and comfort. He is also concerned, at some level, that his perception is, if not inadequate, at least inaccurate. He worries about the fact that he does not perceive or feel as do many of his fellows. His concern is probably justified, since many — if not most — of the problems he has learned stem from a distorted perception, also learned.

(5) The counselee seeks to learn to interact more effectively, more profitably. He finds that people don't like him. He looks around him and sees that others seem to enjoy life and each other more, apparently, than *he* does. Perhaps he is unable to love, or to receive it, or to work. A deficiency in one or more of these is usually enough to precipitate sufficient anxiety to alert him to his deficiencies and hopefully to motivate him to such counseling. Quite simply, the counselee seeks emotional interchange with people, situations, and with the events in his environment.

(6) Finally, the counselee seeks to learn to derive significant meaning from his interactions. He seeks only to profit from his experience, or, as one counselee put it: "I want to be able to use what I live." Now, this ability to derive significant and positive meaning from experience is based upon the capacity to generalize. What the counselor should also understand, however, is that unhealthy, negative, and anxiety-provoking experiences are generalized as well as healthy, positive experiences. Many counselees seek counseling precisely because their capacity to generalize has gotten out of control (anxieties are overwhelming) to the extent that they are quite unable to sort the chaff from the wheat in whatever experiences they undergo.

4

Practical Techniques
in the Initial Contact

There are certain techniques which the counselor can employ to enable him to function more effectively at the initial interview as well as in subsequent ones. These techniques are: handling silences, listening, questioning, reiterating, advising, clarifying, reflecting, and recapitulating.

Silences

Silence in the initial counseling session is not uncommon. It occurs for a variety of reasons and may be a function of shyness, fear, hostility, or anxiety.

Quite understandably, many counselees are inhibited about discussing their personal lives with strangers; and — at least until the end of the first contact — the counselor *is* in effect a "stranger." If the counselor is able to detect that the counselee is not talking for reasons of shyness (considerable blushing, stammering, etc.), he may try relaxing him with a few irrelevant comments, appropriate quips, etc.

Some counselees are afraid to talk. They may be hiding problems which they are too frightened or too embarrassed to discuss, since they are with a stranger. Or perhaps they have learned to be suspicious.

They need time to conclude that they can trust the counselor. The amount of time they need to allay their suspicions, of course, will depend on the quality and the quantity of experiences which engendered and reinforced their fear of strangers.

At times, counselees are referred by a figure perceived by them as an authoritarian (principal, teacher, parent). This perception, together with the hostility attached to it, is often displaced onto the counselor. How long the displacement lasts will, of course, be dependent largely on the personal qualities of the counselor.

Finally, there are counselees who are too anxious to talk. Their anxiety, a product of conflicts, frustrations, etc., is such that they have learned that the safest way to deal with these conflicts and frustrations is to keep quiet about them. Too often this "keeping quiet" has had unfortunately deleterious consequences — namely, the suppression, even repression, of many interpersonal skills. For counselees such as these, the silences may be viewed as the manifestation of interpersonal ineptitude.

How can the counselor deal with the silences? What can he do? There are a number of available possibilities:

(1) He can sit patiently *with* the counselee. Fidgeting, loud sighing, recurrent throat-clearing, etc, by the counselor are inappropriate, since they generally serve only to increase counselee tension.

(2) He can say appropriately, "Mm-hmm,* Uh-huh, Yes," or any other short, positive remark which communicates "Yes, I'm with you; take your time." Such comments serve to recognize sympathetically the counselee's discomfort and difficulty in expressing himself.

(3) The counselor can reiterate the last counselee comment, e.g., "He just threw the eraser at her."

(4) He can add a question to the preceding reiteration: "And then what happened?"

(5) He can summarize the last comments. He might begin the summary as follows: "Now, let's see, Jim; you were saying that —."

(6) He can confront the counselee with the silence: "We're not awfully talkative, are we?"

Whether these suggestions are effective or not is dependent on several variables. These are: (1) the affect and/or tone of voice with which the counselor says "Uh-huh," reiterates, questions, summarizes, etc., (2) how appropriate the particular technique is to the personality of the counselee, and (3) how appropriate the particular technique is to the moment and the counseling climate. All these factors, of course, are dependent on counselor personality, judgment, and experience and

---

* At least one study has shown that the appropriate use of "Mm-hmm" by the counselor can increase counselee speech (Matarazzo, et al. 1964b)

involve some risk, since the counselor does not know the counselee well at this time.

Listening

Patterson (1959) feels that listening is "the basic, most universal, most important technique in counseling and psychotherapy." Whether listening is *the* most important technique or not might be debated, but that a counselee finds the counselor who listens to him psychologically rewarding is fairly obvious. The counselee finds security in being listened to. He feels accepted, and his self-esteem is fed. There is little doubt that effective listening by both participants, but particularly by the counselor, can only enhance the positive aspects of the climate of the initial session.

The student counselor, particularly, frequently has difficulty with the listening technique. Even for many experienced counselors (this author included), it is not easy to remember in an emotionally laden counseling session — as the initial one so often is — not to interrupt the counselee with a question, a bit of advice, or a well-intended supportive remark such as "I know what you mean." It might be helpful in this regard to remember that the counselor's prime function here is to meet counselee needs, not his own. Interruptions, long discourse, opinions, or constant comments by the counselor serve only to communicate counselor pomposity or — worse still — a lack of interest in and concern for the counselee and his problems.

The prime characteristic of the counselor who is a good listener is that he is motivated to listen. He is attentive and focuses on the counselee's words, feelings, and behaviors.

The following list of practical suggestions may help the counselor to communicate his motivation to listen:

(1) He sits in such a way that he can look at the counselee directly. [Quite probably, Freud's method of sitting behind the client was a technique which was more in response to the counselor's needs than to the client's (Freud, 1959).]

(2) The counselor insulates both participants from external distraction — i.e., noise, objects, and interruptions. This counselor once worked in an office which looked out into a corridor. Passing students were a constant source of distraction until a heavy drape was obtained for the windows. Also, the counselor might find that hanging a "Do not disturb" sign on the counseling door will cut down on interruptions.

(3) The counselor seeks to eliminate or ameliorate internal distractions. Thoughts and ideas pertinent to the counselor's personal life,

but irrelevant to the counselee's problems, are, insofar as possible, resisted and suppressed during the counseling hour. Admittedly, this is easier said than done, and for some counselors not easy at all. In any case, the counselor who is aware of ideational intrusions and of the deleterious effect which they can have on his listening will try to resist them.

(4) The counselor is exquisitely sensitive toward and responds appropriately to emotionally charged words. The counselor quickly learns that certain words, themes, and topics have strong meaning for one counselee and no meaning for another.

(5) The counselor notices and responds, if appropriate, to the counselee's grimaces, verbal ejaculations, and bodily movements as behavioral communications. The listener-counselor fully appreciates that for some counselees various physical movements are attempts to communicate various feelings and emotions, such as conflict, rage, fear, joy, etc.

(6) The counselor questions appropriately. As noted below, there are times when questions are entirely appropriate. When used appropriately, questions can reflect not only that a counselor is listening, but also that he is actively listening, an important concern of at least two researchers (Grigg and Goodstein, 1957).

Finally, effective listening has an additionally important value. It helps to achieve understanding; and understanding, according to Rogers (1957), is a prerequisite to ameliorative change. The counselor who can communicate that he is listening is in essence communicating "You have some important things to say"; and, for some counselees, the derivative meaning of this first statement is the second: "You are important." The counselor who can make these dynamic communications at the initial interview will have gone a long way toward establishing rapport. Dynamic communication such as this goes a long way toward promoting counselee feelings of security, acceptance, and self-worth and — equally important — relating to the client that his indigenous perception of the world has value. Moreover, the belief here is that communications such as these can precipitate only "therapeutic understanding" (Patterson, 1959) and effect healthful change.

Questioning

Whether questions are appropriate or inappropriate at the initial interview will be largely dependent on the personalities of the participants. Some counselees are immediately threatened, others apparently respond well to them. Questions for the latter may be very valuable, as they are an easy, quick way to obtain background information, to induce discussions, or to focus the interview. The former, on the other hand, may be driven away by them. Whether questions are used or not, then, will be dependent on the dynamics of the participants, the particular nature of their interaction, and the judgment and experience of the counselor.

Inappropriate Use of Questions

Following is an example of the inappropriate use of questions at an initial interview. The counselee is a high school boy, seventeen years old, and a junior:

Cor: Hi! John S., isn't it?
Cee: Nope. Mike B.
Cor: Oh! Of course. I'm sorry. I was looking at the wrong place in my appointment book. (*Chuckle*) That's me.
Cee: Yeah.

[Pause]

Cor: Well, how are things going?
Cee: Great!

[Pause]

Cor: Yes, uh, Miss Jones, the English teacher, not the math person, uh, seems to feel a little differently.
Cee: So-o-o?
Cor: Uh. Yes. So what happened?
Cee: Nothing.

[Pause]

Cor: Yes. I mean, surely she wouldn't just refer you. I mean, why did she refer you?
Cee: Search me.

The above example includes about as bad a set of questions for an initial interview as could be imagined. First, the counselor commits a most unforgiveable error, namely: not knowing the counselee's name. He thereby communicates at a latent level, "I don't think you're very important." Secondly, the counselor contradicts the counselee: "Miss Jones . . . . feels differently." The counselee could take this to mean that he is a liar. And thirdly, what continues to make the whole initial contact so awkward is the fact that the questions asked often were the kind that an already-peeved client could easily reply to with one-word answers. This probably only delighted him, since it thereby provided him with an opportunity to communicate his resistance, if not his hostility.

Appropriate Use of Questions

Following is an illustration of an appropriate use of questions by a school counselor. The client is a fifteen-year-old sophomore boy:

Cor: Ah. Frank B.? I'm Mr. Williams, the school counselor.
Cee: Yeah.
[Pause]
Cor: (*Chuckle.*) It seems you've been having a little trouble in gym.
[Pause]
Cee: Yeah.
Cor: Want to go over it with me?
[Pause]
Cor: I can appreciate that. (*Chuckle.*) You've already gone over the gym floor —
[Pause]
Cee: (*Silence*)
Cor: You don't especially want to talk about it.
[Pause]
Cee: (*Silence*)
You know all about it anyway.
Cor: Only what I heard from the coach; only *his* side of it; only as *he* sees it. How do *you* see it all?
Cee: Yeah, well — Ah forget it. It don't matter anyway.
Cor: What don't matter?
Cee: Kids and how they get treated here. That don't matter.
Cor: What makes you say that, Frank?
Cee: Why? For Christ's sake! Do you know what I did? Do you know what I did? *All* I did?
Cor: Tell me. What did you do?
Cee: I walked on the gym floor with my shoes on. That's it. That's all of it. There isn't no more. I walked on the gym floor, and that S.O.B. down in the gym yelled at me in front of everybody. So I told him off right in front of everybody. Bastard asked for it. Lousy floor. Big deal. . . . I didn't even get a mark on it, and that's what's so funny about it. Not one lousy mark. "You might've, you might've," he said. You think he owned the damned gym. And, and, it's like that about everybody around here — desks, chairs, even the damned Johns. You can't even go to the John on the second floor between 12:00 and 1:00 because they gotta be washed. For Christ's sake. Sometimes I think this school's here for the janitors, the teachers, the principal, and the gym teacher. It sure isn't here for the kids, at least not the way they run it, it isn't.

The counselee's questions in this second illustration are formed in a climate of warmth, security, and acceptance. How did the counselor create this climate? What, besides the fact that he knew the client's name, did he do or say that melted the client's coldness and hostility? He chuckles, he quips about going over the gym floor, he makes supportive statements, "I can appreciate that," and he re-uses client words such as "especially" and "don't." These chuckles, quips, and words serve to communicate to the counselee that this counselor is not concerned with condemning him or with punishing him. Even more, the counselor's need-satisfying remarks like "only *his* side of it, only as *he* sees it" communicate "Your side is valuable, too," perhaps even "You, too, are valuable." Finally, note the last couple of questions by the counselor: "Why do you say that, Frank?" and "Tell me. What did you do?" These types of questions are conducive to considerable verbal and emotional expression while the first counselor's questions led to one-word or one-phrase answers.

Reiterating

Rewording counselee statements can be a very valuable technique in the initial contact. As noted above, often a counselee does not know why he seeks counseling. He is confused. Reiterating by the counselor alleviates or at least ameliorates counselee confusion (both cognitive and emotional), as it serves to put into words what the counselee is too afraid, too guilty, or too angry to say. By reiterating, the counselor can help the counselee to focus, sharpen, and delineate his thinking. Reiterating can also help the counselee to consider his problems from a different viewpoint.

Reiterating at the first interview, then, is another technique which can help the new counselee to crystalize his thoughts about the nature of his problems and about the new relationship into which he is entering.

The following example illustrates how effective reiterating might be. The counselee is a twenty-three-year-old unwed mother. The setting is a mental hygiene clinic:

(1) CEE: I'm not here because I want to be. I'm here only because the social worker sent me.

(1) COR: The social worker wants you to be here.

(2) CEE: I mean, what am I supposed to get out of this? What can I get out of all this? You're probably going to do what my social worker's doing — nothing. I don't want people prying into my life.

(2) COR: You believe that you're not going to get anything out of all this; and not only that but you will have another person to whom you will have to expose your personal life, particularly your life with your parents and your boy friend.

(3) CEE: You got the picture exactly.

(3) COR: You feel, who needs to be subjected to a lot of snooping around, particularly when it's not going to help. Who needs to uncover a lot of material that would better be left alone, particularly since it's so painful.

(4) CEE: Well, don't get me wrong. It's not that I have anything against you. It's nothing personal. You might be able to help other people.

[SILENCE]

(4) COR: I might be able to help other people but not you. (*Pause.*) It's just that you don't feel that you're like other people.

(5) CEE: Well, that's kind of silly, I suppose, to feel that way. I've always had that feeling, I suppose. But, but —

[PAUSE]

I suppose it's just that I've never been able to trust people. I just can't trust strangers; some people can do that, I can't.

(5) COR: Some people just can't be trusted, or if they can you just don't seem to be able to do it. Look at what happened when you trusted one man. He's made you feel even more like this, that you can't be too trusting.

[PAUSE]

(6) CEE: Yeah. I suppose he has. I was always a little bit more suspicious than I had to be —. Yes, I guess he's made me feel more like this. I suppose he has.

This counselee is quite confused. She is afraid, suspicious, and initially she was quite hostile. Like so many counselees at an initial interview, however, she is receptive to cues of understanding and acceptance. In counselor comment (2) above, the counselor is able to communicate both understanding of the counselee's verbalizations and an acceptance of them. The facility with which the counselor reiterates and crystallizes counselee thinking is seen in counselor statements (4) and (5) above.

Advising

As was noted at the beginning of this monograph, counseling is an interpersonal process. As such, it is very much concerned with the client's dynamic life, i.e., his needs, defenses, perceptions, interactive style, and meaning derivatives. It was also noted that the counselor views the client's anxieties and frustrations with vocation and/or education as a function of these same dynamics. The reader will understand, then, that the counselor advisor or advice-giver could not easily fit into such a view of counseling.

The reader should also understand, however, that there are dynamically oriented counselors who feel that advice-giving is very much in order (Sullivan, 1954; Colby, 1951; and Wolberg, 1954). There are also those who feel that advice should not be given under any circumstances (Ingham and Love, 1954; Arbuckle, 1961.) The author subscribes to Arbuckle's (1961) idea that the counselor "does not offer advice because he does not have any advice to give." Quite simply, the counselor is not an advisor, but a helper; and, as has been noted elsewhere, . . . a counselor is neither omniscient or omnipotent. And he who gives advice necessarily casts himself into the role of deity" (Perez, 1965).

At the same time, let us note that there are many counselors who take the point of view that their work does not concern itself with the dynamics of their client because their work entails disseminating vocational and/or educational information. And admittedly, at an initial interview, simple facts can be disseminated fairly, objectively, and effectively by a counselor oriented to information giving without undue concern for a client's dynamics. But let it be understood and borne in mind that such an individual is not *counseling*, he is disseminating information. To reiterate, counseling involves a knowledge, concern, and understanding of human dynamics.

The counselor concerned with human dynamics quickly becomes aware that often the problem which the counselee presents is not the problem with which he is concerned.* In many of our public schools, for example, the problems presented by the client manifestly may involve planning for an education or choosing a vocation. The dynamically oriented counselor is very much aware that often manifest problems of choice may be a symptom of latent dynamic problems. Most certainly, such choices invariably contain emotional overtones and decisions are influenced by the counselee's personality make-up.

Now, this is *not* to say that at every initial interview the dynamically oriented counselor sees each client as one who needs counseling. (This is particularly true in the school setting where many clients are authoritatively or automatically referred periodically.) This *is* to say, however, that at every initial (and subsequent) interview this counselor perceives and relates to his client as one who needs *not* advice, but one who needs to feel secure, accepted, worthy, and free. Moreover, this counselor approaches the initial interview with the understanding that subsequent counseling will be dependent on the climate created by the interaction of their respective dynamics (Van der Veen, 1965).

Two examples follow,† in which the counselor is involved with the

---

* See section below: "Problems: Manifest and Covert."
† For reasons of space, these examples have been abbreviated considerably.

dissemination of information. The first counselor is advice-oriented, the second is dynamically oriented:

COUNSELOR I

COR: Ah, John, Come in, come in. Good to see you.

CEE: Hello, Mr. B. I'm sorry I'm late, but I —

COR: It's all right, it's all right. I understand about those things. I make mistakes too. Nobody's perfect. Well, we've got a few minutes before the bell, anyway. Tell you why you're here. I'm seeing all the seniors twice this year, just to be sure that they have plans made for college or what-have-you. What have you been doing about it?

CEE: Well, to tell the truth, I haven't done very much of anything.

COR: Well, that's all right. I can appreciate that. Don't let it worry you. We'll work out something. That's what I'm here for, to help.

CEE: Uh —

COR: Now, what have you decided? Are you going to college or not?

CEE: Well, to tell the truth I don't know.

COR: What seems to be the trouble?

CEE: I'm not sure if I can go or not — I mean, I'm not that hot a student, and I really don't know what I can do if I don't go.

COR: You're confused about the whole business.

CEE: Yes, I guess I am.

COR: Well, don't feel bad. You've got plenty of company.

[PAUSE]

So let's look at your record. (*Scrutinizing the record.*) Well, your grades are fair to good, I'd say. Your IQ is very good.

CEE: What is it?

COR: Well, I can't tell you that. You understand.

CEE: Yeah, sure . . .

COR: I can tell you that you're brighter than most of the kids in your class. I'd say you were bright enough to make it in the Ivy League. Unfortunately, you haven't got the grades.

CEE: Yeah, well that I know.

COR: Yes. Well, of course you have performed quite well on your achievements in Algebra and Biology. You're way up over the 80th percentile in both subjects. That means that over 80 percent of the kids who took this test scored below you.

CEE: Yeah, I liked those subjects. English and Languages hurt me, in grades I mean.

Cor: Yes. You did poorly on those. We don't have to go into those.

CEE: Yeah, I'm sure. What should I do?

COR: Well, really it's not for me to advise you. Uh, let's look at your vocational tests here. It shows that you are interested in outdoor work.

CEE: Well, I like outdoor work. I was a lifeguard for the past two summers. But I don't think I'd like to be a lifeguard all my life.

COR: (*Chuckle.*) No, I guess not. What would you like to do?

CEE: Search me.

COR: What do your parents say about all this?

CEE: They want me to go to college.

COR: Uh-huh.

CEE: They've always wanted me to go to college. That's all I've heard ever since grammar school: How I had to go to college, just like Dad, good old Dad.

COR: Yes. Well, I'm sure that they're interested only in your future. That's true of most parents. They want you to file for college. They don't want you to be left out. We can't blame them for that, now, can we?

CEE: Yeah.

COR: Look. You think all this over — and come back, let's say, in the middle of next week during one of your free periods; and we'll talk about it. Don't let me have to call you, now —

[FOUR-WEEK INTERVAL]

COR: Ah, John. I'm so glad you came back.

CEE: Hello.

COR: So what have you decided?

CEE: Not very much, really.

COR: Well, you know, John; really, it *is* getting late. I mean, if you're going to apply to college, we have to get the applications in.

CEE: Yeah, I know. My folks are driving me crazy telling me that.

COR: Yes. Well, they *are* your parents and are interested only in you.

CEE: Yeah. Well, I don't know what to do, so I guess we'd better send in applications to the University and to the junior college here in town.

COR: Wonderful! I'll have the secretary type them out today, and I'll call your father for the checks to go with them. He'll be pleased, I know.

CEE: Yeah.

COR: And thanks for coming in — You're a nice boy.

The impression one has of this counselor is that he is not so much interested in meeting John's needs as he is in getting him filed for college or involved in an occupational choice. Quite obviously, John resists the idea of filing for college. This resistance probably stems from problems at home, problems — possibly — with "good old Dad." But this counselor was not attuned to John's dynamics so much as he was to "getting his job done," namely: getting every senior involved in an educational or vocational choice.

COUNSELOR II

This second example illustrates how the dynamically oriented counselor might handle this same John:

[FIRST SESSION]

COR: Come in, John. Come in.

CEE: I'm sorry I'm late, Mr. C; but I was in study hall and forgot the time.

COR: Really involved in your studies, huh?

CEE: Well, not as much as I probably ought to be.

COR: You don't feel you're involved as much as you ought to be.

CEE: No, I'm not.

COR: How do you feel about it?

CEE: Well, finally I'm starting to get a little worried. This is my last year. I know you're calling all the seniors in, to find out what we're going to do for college. That's why I was called in, right?

COR: Yes.

CEE: Well, I'll level with you. I just don't know *what* to do, whether I should apply to college or go to work or what.

COR: You're sort of confused about the whole business.

CEE: To say the least.

[PAUSE]

And I'm driving my folks crazy because I haven't made any decision.

COR: How do you feel about that?

CEE: About driving them crazy? (*Chuckle.*) I don't know

[PAUSE]

It's just that all I've heard ever since grammar school was how I had to go to college, just like Dad — good old Dad.

COR: You don't feel you should go to college just because your father went.

CEE: No, 'course not. I mean, for Christ's sake; sometimes I think that they're not interested in me — just in my going to college. You know what I mean?

COR: Yes, I do. You feel sometimes that they want you to go to college to please them; maybe so they'll get some status out of it, perhaps.

CEE: Right.

[PAUSE]

The hell with them!

[PAUSE]

COR: You don't feel that they accept you for yourself. So this is one way to get back at them.

[PAUSE]

CEE: Well, I don't know if that's so.

[PAUSE]

Let me think about it.

[THREE-DAY INTERVAL]

CEE: I'm back.

COR: Oh, good. Sit down, John.

CEE: I only got a minute. I'm in between classes.

COR: Yes.

CEE: Uh, I want you to know I wrote for applications to a couple of colleges; and I wanted to ask, could you send my transcripts to the University and the junior college?

COR: Of course. Glad to.

CEE: (*Getting up to go.*) Yeah. Well, I was thinking about what we talked about. No point in biting off your nose to spite your face.

COR: You mean you feel you might be hurting yourself more in the long run than you would be your parents.

CEE: Yeah. That's probably right.

Admittedly, the examples here are abbreviated and over-simplified. But the principle involved is neither. Human beings respond when interest in them is displayed. Adolescents, particularly, are exquisitely sensitive and often hostile to the individual who perceives them not as people with needs but as applications to be processed.

This second counselor's focus was John, not the college application. And John responded to this. Quite simply, the high school senior counselee is very much aware that he is supposed to file an application for college. The problem is not a cognitive one but an emotional one. John feels, in part anyway, that his parents — and probably the adult world — are impervious to him as a person. Their concern, he feels, is with his performance, not with him. The counselor focuses on *him*. John responds.

Clarification and Reflection of Feeling

Canon (1964) has observed that counseling involves something more than an emotional interchange between participants. This may be true. The position here, however, is that the counselor who is sensitive to, seeks to understand and appropriately react to, counselee affect is one who will be a more effective counselor. To a very great extent, clients seek counseling because, at some level, they become aware of the fact that their feelings are unmanageable, inappropriate, and confusing to them. They find they can not love others or accept love. They are disturbed because they are unable to control their anger or perhaps that they never get angry when they feel they should. It may be that they are beset by a constant seething hatred which they cannot fathom. Quite simply, they do not understand their feelings, and they want to.

It is at the initial interview that the counselor must communicate his sensitivity, his acceptance, and his understanding of the counselee's feelings. If the counselor is unable to do this, he will doubtless encounter difficulty. It is unfortunate but true that inappropriate reaction to counselee feelings is often construed by the counselee as a rejection of him. To many a counselee, the simple emotional belief is: "Not to accept and deal with my feelings is not to accept and deal with *me*." The reason for this is quite understandable. Feelings are attached to words, to behavior, and — indeed — in most cases they are the *raison d'etre* for both words and behavior. And so, the communication to many counselees is that if the counselor does not accept and deal with my feelings, he is not accepting and dealing with me.

There are two techniques which the counselor can use to help the counselee to better understand and effectively manage his feelings. These are clarification and reflection.

Clarification

In clarification, the counselor deals with the cognitive, intellectual side of the counselee's words. To do this, the counselor explains the meaning which the counselee's words have for both participants. The counselor's object is to get at the client's emotions via words rather than feelings. In doing this the counselor is careful not to explain too much too quickly, since he is ever mindful that an understanding of one's feelings is a complex, slow, and often painful process.

Reflection

In reflection, the counselor deals with the emotional or feeling side of the counselee's words. He is concerned with the emotional under-currents of the counselee's verbalizations. In reflection, the counselor reads between the lines, as it were, and responds to unexpressed attitudes as well as the emotions underlying thought content. The counselor accomplishes all this by using in his response the counselee's words, the counselee's tones, and by attempting to achieve the counselee's feelings.

Clarification and Reflection in an Initial Interview

The following excerpts from an initial interview may help to illustrate the use of these two techniques. The client is a twenty-two-year-old married college man who is having marital difficulties. The setting is a college counseling center. The first excerpt illustrates clarification:

(1) CEE: Yeah, well it's just that she's not even interested in being a wife. I mean, I have a philosophy about these things. All she has to do is take care of one room — one little room in my mother's house. And she can't even do that. My philosophy is that she ought to learn to do it — I mean, this is her job, to take care of the room and be a wife to me. Take care of what belongs to us. I mean, if she won't do that, take care of one lousy room, how's she going to take care of an apartment and maybe someday a house, if she can't even take care of one, lousy little room.

(1) COR: Yes. Your feeling is that your wife should adapt, expend some energy to adapt to being a wife. If she's not even trying to do that when the demands are minimal, how can she do it when the demands increase as they surely will.

(2) CEE: Right. I come home at night to study after classes and working a job and everything, and I find her sitting on her derrière reading the paper while my mother, who's getting on in years now, is

ironing my shirts. I mean, that's not my mother's job — she's got enough to do. It's *her* job, not my mother's.

(2) Cor: Yes. Your feeling is that it's a wife's job to iron her husband's shirts. Your mother's maternal responsibilities should have ended with your marriage.

(3) Cee: That's right, exactly. But my poor mother's load wasn't lightened; it just increased when that lazy bitch came into our house.

(3) Cor: Your mother didn't lose a son and she didn't gain a daughter — she only took in a boarder.

(4) Cee: You hit it right on the head. Right. And I can tell you even more —.

Note in each exchange above (1, 2, and 3) how the client assents to the counselor's explanations and interruptions. The assent denotes not only an agreement but an acceptance of the counselor's attempt at clarification. The counselee's expansion after a counselor clarification is usually a pretty good sign that the counselor is communicating effectively.

The following excerpts with the same client, during the same interview, illustrate use of the reflection technique:

Cee: — And I can tell you even more. I know she's running around, I know she is. I know I'm not a helluva lot to look at, and I know she is.

[Pause]

Cor: Hm-m-m. You feel she's a helluva lot more to look at as a woman than you are as a man.

Cee: I know it. I know it. Everybody thinks she's a doll. And she is. She's — also a cheap little two-timer.

Cor: Even though people think she's a doll, you feel she's a cheap little two-timer.

Cee: Right.

[Pause]

See, the whole problem here is a simple one. I married beneath me. She's really a lower-class girl, just a lower-class girl. Her father drives a garbage truck for the city, and her mother's an alcoholic from way back. She was working in a factory when I met her.

Cor: She's a lower-class girl with an alcoholic mother and a father who drives a garbage truck.

Cee: Right.

Cor: You wonder how in God's name you're in the situation you're in today — Married to a girl who's only virtue is that she's a doll, but who's cheap, a two-timer, and lower-class to boot.

Cee: Right. God, what am I going to do? I can't divorce her; my parents would have kittens — even though they don't think much of her. I'm a Catholic in name only, but my mother, especially, is very devout.

Cor: Right now you're pretty confused and worried. Divorce would pose all kinds of problems for everybody, especially your mother who's extremely devout.

The reader should observe the counselor's use of the word "feel" and his re-use of the counselee's words. It is in these ways that the counselor attempts to get at the emotions underlying the counselee's verbalizations. It is in these ways that he attempts to communicate an understanding of the client's feelings.

Often the counselor will find it advantageous to use both clarification and reflection. The excerpts which follow are with the same client and illustrate how a counselor can clarify and reflect simultaneously:

CEE: And then what makes it all so much worse is that I can't even talk to her. She's always so damned quiet, "withdrawn" is a better word. She's withdrawn, but only in the house. She's a real hell-raiser at a party.

COR: She's a hell-raiser at a party, but at home she's quite uncommunicative.

CEE: Uncommunicative is the word, right. She goes into our bedroom and naps, reads, combs her hair, and tends to herself. Bothers with no one. She never comes out to chat. If I go in there to talk to her, she gets mad or she sulks. She's, she's, a nut. I don't know what the hell to do.

COR: You feel she spends too much time on herself. She won't let you talk to her. You're confused.

CEE: Yes, I am that. I'm confused.
[PAUSE]
If only we could talk. But she won't. You have to talk. I mean, no wonder she's such a nut — she just won't let anybody near her even to talk.

COR: She won't let anybody near her, not even you — her husband.

CEE: Right.
[PAUSE]
We haven't had relations twice in the past three months.
[PAUSE]
I mean, what the hell kind of marriage is that?

COR: You feel that a good sign that your marriage has fallen apart is the fact that you haven't had relations twice in the past three months.

CEE: Right. I mean, what else can I conclude?

Recapitulating

The client, at an initial interview particularly, may launch into a long, unfocused discourse. The reasons for this may vary with the client and — more particularly — with his perception of the counselor and/or the counseling situation. He may be afraid, suspicious, or his general anxiety may be so strong that he can't focus his thoughts.

The rambling discourse may be viewed as the counselee's way of keeping the counselor at a distance while he determines just how tolerant, accepting, and trustworthy the counselor is. The long discourse may also be viewed by the potential counselor as a verbal smoke screen employed by the insecure counselee to camouflage the insecurity he feels in this new and unique situation of counseling.

Whatever the reasons for them, long, ruminating, and rambling discourses by the counselee *do* occur. Now, what can the counselor do about them? Quite simply, he can recapitulate. Recapitulating refers to the simple technique of *tying and connecting* unorganized and ill-arranged material from the counselee's discourse. By recapitulating, the counselor helps the counselee to focus on the basic theme or topic of his discourse. Whenever possible, the counselor uses counselee words and phrases. Under no circumstances does the counselor introduce a new topic or theme.

The following excerpts from an initial interview illustrate this technique of recapitulating. The client is a twenty-nine-year-old unmarried woman. The problem she presents centers around the anxiety she experiences whenever she seeks to leave her parents' home and obtain her own apartment:

CEE: Well, it isn't that I don't think he's sharp, because in his own way I guess he is. He is sharp, my father; it's just that he lets my mother walk all over him. He does. He lets her walk all over him. And I know, too, 'cause I know him. I ought to — I've been living with him for twenty-nine years. Twenty-nine years! Imagine that if you can! For twenty-nine years my mother has been pushing him around. Walking all over him. He doesn't work. He stopped working, uh, I remember, when I was in the seventh grade. Let's see, that must have been sixteen or seventeen years ago because I was only twelve. Lord, how that woman has debased him! Why, even as a child I couldn't stand watching it! Don't get me wrong now, maybe she had reasons for acting like she did; and I have to admit that Mom *is* overworked, underpaid, and — I suppose — unappreciated. But her trouble is that she shows all three, if you know what I mean. She shows all three. Now, did I confuse you? I'll bet I did!

COR: Uh, you said a lot! (*Chuckle.*) Uh, you've been living with your folks for twenty-nine years. You feel your mother's been, uh, pushing him around, walking all over him as it were, and even debasing him. This bothered you as a child. Perhaps the strain of trying to understand all this is what leads you to want to leave home and set up your own apartment.

CEE: Yes, maybe you're right. I *do* want to leave. That's what I came here for — to find out why I can't when it comes down to doing it. Lord knows I want to. It's just that my brother keeps making me feel, how can I describe it, makes me feel, uh, I suppose you'd say worried, guilty — yes, guilty. (*Chuckle.*) But he's a worry, Albert. He's twenty-three. Works for a used car dealer, and he's been trying to talk my mother into a new car. A new car! Imagine, and she's got all she can do with her pay and my thirty dollars a week to support herself and the house. He just hasn't got any judgment, that brother of mine. None. He's got none. Yes, if only he'd do what I told him to do: get Dad a job at that place where he works. Not that he could sell cars, because he couldn't do that in a hundred years. He couldn't. But I'm sure he could get a sweeper's job. He's handy. He can do all sorts of jobs. I know. And it's the biggest dealership around. If Albert wanted to, he could. He just doesn't want to. Am I talking too much? Yes, I am.

COR: Uh. You'd like to leave home, but your brother doesn't seem too responsible and, uh, makes you feel like your thirty dollars are really needed at home. And, uh, if your father worked then, uh, then you could feel like you could leave home. Which is, uh, what you are here for — to find out why you don't leave home.

CEE: Yes, uh, that's right. That's what I came for, isn't it? I do. Yes, I do want to leave home. Why can't I? Tell me, why can't I? I suppose they're all a little responsible and me, too.

COR: Do you feel they're all responsible?

CEE: Yes. Yeah, I do. My brother makes me feel, uh, guilty. My mother keeps doing things to my father. And she knows it. She knows it bothers me. And my father — he won't get off his behind and go to work to help out.

What this excerpt shows is an unusually acute ability of the counselor (a friend of this author) to take the most meaningful points of a long counselee discourse and recapitulate them. The recapitulation has the effect of focusing the counselee's thoughts on her central problem which, in part at least, she wants to escape.

Problems: Manifest and Covert

Often the problems which clients present are not those which trouble them. Bordin (1955) has found that what they present as their problem is related to how they perceive their counselor. This finding is supported by Grater (1964) who found that "the characteristics the counselee considers significant in the counselor are indicative of the type of problem the counselee will discuss." What problems the counselee will discuss is determined in large measure by the counselor's personality characteristics and style of participation (Rice, 1965).

What the reader should know, then, is that often manifest problems are only symptoms of other problems, and these usually are more serious. Equally important, the prospective counselor should be aware that his own value system with its attached communication scheme will inhibit or precipitate discussion of the real and covert problem. A counselor who is basically morally punitive is not likely to get the high schooler who came in manifestly to discuss a change in college choice to discuss her illegitimate pregnancy. And let us note that the high schooler who is in such a predicament will be exquisitely sensitive to any and all punitive or judgmental cues which deal with social and moral standards.

Characteristics of Counselee with Covert Problem

The following list contains some of the more common characteristics found in the counseling session where the counselee seeks to keep his problem covert:

(1) Rambling, unfocused discussion after a statement of the problem.

(2) An apparent unwillingness to leave the counseling office.

(3) Long pauses or an uncommon number of silences.

(4) An apparent hostility toward conventional morality, religion, or clergy, people perceived as overly rigid or judgmental.

(5) An inability to begin talking or to explain what his problem is.

(6) A wide disparity between the apparent degree of counselee discomfort and the problem he presents.

The Counselor's Role with Covert Problems

Now, what can the counselor do, what behavior should he display, what words can he use to help the client to discuss his real problem more willingly? There are a number of techniques which he can employ to help combat each of the above evidences of covert counselee problems:

(1) Rambling, unfocused discussion after a statement of the problem.

As noted above, periodic recapitulation by the counselor may help the counselee to gain or regain his thought trends. Sometimes it also may be well to patiently let such a counselee ramble for the better part of the session, and then let him know before the interview is completed that you feel he might have something else that is bothering him; for example, "Uh, somehow after all this, I have the feeling that you might have something else which is troubling you," or "I don't mean to pry, you understand." How directly or indirectly the question is posed will, of course, depend on the judgment of the counselor, how effectively he gauges the moment, and the personalities of both participants.

(2) An apparent unwillingness to leave the counseling office.

This is usually a sure sign that the counselee has something else on his mind. Behavior such as this may be interpreted as a plea by the counselee, a plea to be confronted with the question "What else do you have on your mind?"

(3) Long pauses or an uncommon number of silences.

See section under "Silence" above.

(4) An apparent hostility toward conventional morality, religion, clergy, or people perceived as overly rigid or judgmental.

Reflections and clarifications appropriately made are usually effective. Tolerance is a prime consideration in all dealings with the counselee, but it becomes a critical necessity in the clarifications and reflections made with the client who harangues about morality, religion, and rigidity. The counselor should strive to communicate his concern for the client's need for freedom.

(5) An inability to begin talking or to explain what his problem is.

See section under "Silence" above.

The counselor may seek to relax the counselee by discussing a non-threatening topic, i.e., the weather, or an athletic contest. Also, an appropriate quip or silly joke may have a beneficial effect. It is important to note that the effective employment of such techniques is always dependent on counselor judgment, and how effectively he evaluates himself, the counselee, and the particular interactive climate.

(6) A wide disparity between the apparent degree of counselee discomfort and the problem he presents.

Quite obviously, the counselee who begins weeping after discussing his inability to perform adequately in physical education has related more basic problems. Clarification, reflection, asking, or simple listening are often appropriate here.

Finally, let us note that in each of the above situations the counselee is seeking to communicate but is blocked by anxieties, frustration, fears, etc. His plea, consciously or unconsciously, is for the counselor to help him talk. Refusal to do so may be interpreted by the counselee as a hostile act by the counselor. The counselor's awareness of this fact should assist him in helping the counselee to a more effective first interview.

The Question of Referrals

Following initial contact, one or both of the participants may feel that referral to another counselor is desirable. Some of the reasons for referral are as follows:

(1) Time or scheduling factors
(2) A clash in personalities
(3) Physical or biological problems
(4) The nature of the problem
(5) Differences in theoretical orientations
(6) Ethics or values of the participants

(1) *Time or Scheduling Factors.* At the first interview the counselor may learn that he can not meet the counselee's time requirements. The counselee, for example, might want two, three, or more sessions per week. The counselor himself might feel that the counselee's problem requires several sessions per week. The counselor's schedule, however, might permit him only one session per week. Similarly, in the high school situation, the schedules of the client and the particular counselor may not permit easy or convenient interviews. In such cases, a referral at the end of the first interview is entirely appropriate.

(2) *Clash in Personalities.* Counselors can not be expected to be attracted to or even to work with every client. In fact, from time to time the counselor may find that he is threatened unduly by a particular client. This is not unusual and is to be expected. The counselor learns quickly that there are some clients with whom he can work only with difficulty. The counselor in the psychiatric hospital might find the paranoid schizophrenic acceptable; the character disorder, unacceptable. The high school counselor might find the rowdy adolescent an interesting client, the depressed teener boring. Similarly, the counselor in a child guidance clinic might find it preferable to work with an eneuretic rather than a marginal schizophrenic. Thus, while it can be argued that flexibility in a counselor's preference for a client is necessary, it should be noted also that a counselor is entitled to his likes and dislikes. In any case, if the counselor finds at the close of the first session that he is unduly threatened by the client's personality disposition, he might consider referral. If the threat or clash in dynamics continues to the close of a second session, referral to another counselor is necessary.

(3) *Physical or Biological Problems.* The counselor might find that he can work better with women than with men, better with the exceptional child than with the normal. He might find considerably more emotional and professional reward working with the geriatric than the middle-aged. He may also find that clients of one race are easier and less threatening to work with than those of another. Occasional referral because of the problems the counselor has with the sex, intellectual level, age, or race of the client is not unjustified.

(4) *Nature of the Problem.* If the counselor feels that his training is not adequate to meet the client's problem, he should refer him. If

the client's problems center around a topic which the counselor himself finds painful — e.g., the counselor has just been divorced and finds the client's conflict involves acute marital problems which might culminate in divorce — the counselor should refer him.

(5) *Differences in Theoretical Orientations.* On occasion, the client may be seeking a counselor of particular orientation, i.e., analytic, nondirective, directive. He finds that this counselor is of a different persuasion and asks to be referred. Or it may happen that the counselor feels that a different orientation would be more suitable to a particular client. Admittedly, this is rare, since most counselors unfortunately feel that their particular approach is *the* correct one.

(6) *Ethics or Values.* Not uncommonly, a counselee may inquire about the counselor's ethical system. He may want to know how the counselor feels about the existence of God, marriage, pre- or extramarital sex, etc. The counselee deserves an answer to all of these. If the answers are not to his liking, he may seek to be referred. Less frequently, and hopefully quite rarely, the counselor may feel that his own value system can interfere with the development and maturation of a professional relationship.

Timing may be a critical factor in referrals. Transfer of a counselee should be accomplished as early in the sequence of interviews as possible to minimize complications stemming from the termination of an established relationship. Many clients come to experience feelings of rejection if transferral is delayed too long.

Terminating the Interview

The client should learn at the initial interview that every session has a closing time that must be adhered to. In the public schools, this poses little problem, as the counselor can arrange his sessions to coincide with the established bell system. And in most cases the bell seems to be an adequate enough stimulus; for — as most counselors have observed — public school students have been pretty well conditioned to move with the sound of the bell! If the counselor finds a student going overtime, he should not hesitate to discretely inform the client that the time is up.

In the hospital, mental health clinic, etc., other means might have to be employed for the client who does not respond to the more obvious cues. For example, the counselor might find it convenient to pre-arrange with a secretary to have her knock at the door or announce on the intercom that the next client is waiting. In this regard also, a clock placed in easy view of both participants might be helpful.

Sometimes clients appear to begin to deliver some of their more meaningful material only moments before the end of the hour. To let such clients continue overtime is to teach certain of them, anyway, to be manipulative and/or that they may ramble and ruminate on irrelevancies, if they so desire. Also, to let certain clients continue overtime is to communicate to them that counseling time is not too valuable; not to let certain clients continue overtime is to communicate to them that counseling time is precious.

Even if it appears that one session is all that is needed, it is wise to let the client know that he is welcome to return. Comments like "Keep in touch," or "Let me know how you do," are enough to communicate that the counseling door is open for future interviews.

When the interview is over and the patient has left, the counselor should make some notes as to what transpired. Information such as name, date, sex, address, and referral source should of course be recorded, preferably by a secretary. Even more important, the manifest problem as presented by the client and the counselor's impressions of the client should be noted.

Under no circumstances should such a form be filled out by the counselor during the interview hour. To do so is to take the counselor's full attention away from the client. Moreover, to fill out a form while the client is present is to communicate to the client: "What I get down here is more important than relating to you." Quite simply, to relate to the client via a piece of paper is *never* appropriate.

If the counselor in an outpatient clinic or in private practice finds that he has not picked up particular details during the initial interview, i.e., age, home address, telephone, he can ask the client to stop at the secretary's desk, where a secretary by pre-arrangement can ask for these particular items. The school counselor can get these particular items from the records office.

5

Summary

The initial counseling contact is crucial because it determines if there will be subsequent sessions.

Counseling is viewed in this monograph as an interactive process in which the counselor seeks to help the client deal more effectively with reality. Ideally, the counselor will be dynamically oriented. This means that he will be aware of the fact that both he and the client have needs and defenses. Needs are identical but may vary in level or degree. The defenses may or may not be similar. The counselor is also aware of the crucial importance of his own and the client's perceptual and interactive mode and meaning derivatives.

The setting for counseling is important. The indications are that the counselor who functions in a bare, poorly lighted, shabby room is not likely to get as good results as one who works in an office which is well-lighted, adequately furnished, and generally attractive.

The counselor builds and maintains rapport by dynamically communicating to the client: "I would like very much to come to understand and even share your view of the world." The counselor is a real-life person who seeks only to meet — never to damage — the client's needs of security, acceptance, worthiness, and freedom. The counselor helps to meet these needs, as he strives to be tactful, respectful, tolerant, and rewarding.

For many a counselee the initial interview is seen as an opportunity to obtain a model with whom to identify. There are all sorts of meanings attached to this, most of them positive. The counselor who is aware of such a need in the client and utilizes this knowledge effectively will better meet the client's needs. Conversely, the counselor who seeks to identify with client after client probably has too many problems of his own to function as a counselor. Simple liking of the client, however, can help facilitate the counseling.

Whether or not the counselor structures is dependent on his own and the client's need state, defense patterns, and general perceptions. Structure should not emanate from the counselor's needs but rather from those of the client.

Communication is *a*, if not *the*, central issue in counseling and may occur on a verbal (simple or complex) and on a behavioral level.

Research and current thought indicate that the counselee has traits which set him apart from the individual who does not seek counseling. The indications are that the counselee is less judgmental and more intuitive. However, the indications are also that counselees are individuals who labor under considerable anxiety. From this anxiety devolve feelings of low self-esteem, fear, guilt, resentment, suspicion, and helplessness. The effect of these six feelings is to precipitate weakness in client expression and mode of relating. For example, not uncommonly clients discuss their problems in a long, extraneous way or — worse still — not at all; or they exaggerate and may be quite inaccurate.

Four counselees were asked to consider two questions: Why do you seek counseling? and What do you expect to get out of it? The responses to these questions indicated that:

(1) The counselee suffers from vague, ill-defined, but very real tensions and anxieties.

(2) The counselee seeks to be independent.

(3) The counselee seeks to acquire self-knowledge and understanding.

(4) The counselee seeks to relearn a new and more effective perception of the world generally and his reality in particular.

(5) The counselee seeks to learn to interact more effectively and more profitably.

(6) The counselee seeks to learn to derive significant meaning from his interaction.

Like any other human being, the counselor seeks to feel secure, accepted, worthy, and free. The research indicates that, among other qualities, the counselor seeks to be "warm and passionate, intuitive, and psychologically penetrating." It was noted that any qualities which the particular counselor possesses are important since these qualities determine not only what techniques the counselor will employ but how effective his techniques will be. And in addition, the most important technique which the counselor can employ is an effective personality style, since the indications are that the client is interested in the counselor-person, not in his techniques.

Five practicing counselors were asked to respond to the question "With what thoughts, what feelings, do you approach the initial counseling contact?" Their responses indicated that:

(1) The counselor is concerned, interested, and cares about.the counseling relationship.

(2) The counselor seeks to emotionally invest in the relationship.

(3) Despite this emotional investment, the counselor is cognitively detached.

(4) The counselor is a sensitive person and is aware of the subtlety of the various communicative modes.

(5) The counselor is an introspective person.

The silence in counseling is not uncommon and is a function of the counselee's shyness, hostility, or acute anxiety. How effective the counselor is with the various techniques discussed above depends on several variables. These are: (1) the counselor's affect, (2) how suitable the particular technique is to the personality of the counselee, and (3) how appropriate the particular technique is to the moment and the counseling climate. Counselor personality, judgment, and experience are also critical in managing and understanding silence.

Other practical techniques discussed included: listening, questioning, reiterating, advising, clarifying, reflecting, and recapitulating. The counselor can communicate his desire to listen if he (1) sits appropriately, (2) cuts down on external distractions, (3) eliminates internal distractions, (4) deals appropriately with emotionally charged words, (5) deals appropriately with behavioral cues, and (6) questions appropriately.

Whether questions are used or not will be dependent on the dynamics of the participants, the particular nature of the interaction, and the judgment and experience of the counselor.

Reiterating by the counselor helps to alleviate, or at least ameliorate, counselee confusion (both cognitive and emotional), as it serves to put into words what the counselee feels too afraid, guilty, or angry to say. In addition, reiterating by the counselor can help the counselee to focus, sharpen, and delineate his thinking.

The view presented here is that the advice-giver has no place in dynamic counseling. More often than not, the advice-giver seeks to meet his own needs and not those of the client.

In clarification of feeling, the counselor deals with the cognitive, intellectual side of the counselee's words. The object here is to get at the client's emotions via words rather than feelings. In reflection, the counselor deals with the emotional or feeling side of the counselee's words. Also, in reflection, the counselor is concerned with the emotional undercurrents of the counselee's verbalizations.

A long, ruminating, and rambling talk by the counselee is not uncommon at the initial interview. Such talk can be brought into focus by recapitulating. Recapitulating refers to the simple technique of tying and connecting the unorganized and ill-arranged material from the counselee's discourse. By recapitulating, the counselor can help the counselee to focus on his basic theme or topic.

Often the problems which the client presents are not those which trouble him. This occurs because not uncommonly the problems presented are no more than a symptom of other, more covert, and usually more serious problems. Many times the counselee who has such problems communicates this fact indirectly to the counselor. There are techniques which the counselor can employ to help the client discuss these covert, real problems. Some of these techniques are recapitulating, reflecting, and clarifying.

There are instances in which referral to another counselor is desirable. Six reasons are considered. These are: (1) time or scheduling factors, (2) a clash in personalities, (3) physical or biological factors, (4) the nature of the problem, (5) differences in theoretical orientations, and (6) ethics or values of the participants. Referral should be accomplished as soon as feasible to avoid resentment and discouragement of the counselee.

Finally, the client should learn at the initial session that every session has a closing time that must be adhered to. To let some clients continue overtime is to teach them to be manipulative and to indicate that they may ramble and ruminate if they wish.

APPENDIX A

An Initial Counseling Interview

A sample unedited initial interview is presented in Appendix A. This initial interview transcript will permit the reader to apply the principles and techniques discussed in the preceding chapters. The interview is presented without comment by the counselor or author. It presents the uninterrupted flow of counseling interaction rather than excerpts illustrative of specific points as in the material presented in earlier chapters.

Additionally, a summary of the interview by the counselor is found in Appendix B.

*This is a nineteen-year-old college sophomore who is self-referred.
The setting is a college counseling center.*

COR: Ah, Good morning, Mary. Come in, come in.

CEE: Good morning, doctor.

[PAUSE.]

COR: I haven't seen you since freshman year, have I? I'm glad to see you.

CEE: Well, I'm glad to be here, too. I'm having an awful time at home. I simply have to talk to somebody. It's my mother. She's got me so I can't do anything right. I can't study, I can't date. I can't do anything right any more. She's driving me crazy.

COR: Your mother is driving you crazy.

CEE: Yes — she is. I just don't know what to do. We've never gotten along, but now it's ridiculous. I mean, I can't study at home. She's impossible, just impossible.

[PAUSE.]

COR: You just can't study at home because your mother acts how?

CEE: Well, it's hard to explain. She's just picking on me — and not just me but all of us; well, all of us, but me the most, I guess. She's always picked on me the most. I think she gets positive delight from picking on me. She picks on me about my room, she picks on me about the way I wear my hair, about the clothes I wear. She's always snooping in my room. She reads my mail; I have no privacy. I'm a big girl now. She calls it "mothering me." She's driving me crazy.

COR: You resent your mother's meddling in your life. You feel you're old enough to run your own life now.

CEE: I'm nineteen years old. I'm a sophomore in college. How old do I have to be before I can be treated like an adult? She still thinks of me as if I were ten years old. She even lays out my clothes. Imagine! The night before, she lays out my clothes!

COR: You don't like being treated like a ten-year-old.

CEE: No, I don't.

COR: You feel she should treat you like an adult. You don't need your clothes laid out.

CEE: Heavens no!

[SILENCE.]

COR: You don't need to be treated like a ten-year-old.

CEE: (*Sighs.*) No, I don't.

[SILENCE.]

COR: You're very upset, Mary.

CEE: Yes, I am. She's just driving me crazy. (*Bursts into tears.*)

COR: I see.

[PAUSE.]

CEE: God. I can't do any work. I'm almost failing in two courses! I came here as an honor student. I was always a good student. I'm barely staying in school. I don't seem to be able to study any more.

COR: Hm-m-m. Studying has become a problem.

CEE: I don't have a place to study anymore. My mother used to be interested in how I did in school. When I was going to high school she used to ask me if I did my homework. She doesn't anymore. It just doesn't matter to her anymore if I've done it or not. She just picks, picks, picks at me.

COR: What you're saying is that you're upset that she doesn't care whether you've done your homework or not. She picks on you about other things but doesn't seem concerned about that.

CEE: Yeah.

COR: Why doesn't she pick on you about your homework?

CEE: She does.

COR: She does?

CEE: Yeah. But she won't let me do it.

COR: She won't let you do it? Why not?

CEE: I just don't have a place to do it anymore.

COR: You don't?

CEE: No. (*Pause.*) My aunt came to live with us last year.

COR: So-o-o-o?

CEE: She's got my room now. I don't have a place to study. It's all her fault when you come down to it. I have to sleep on the couch in the living room. I've had to now for almost nine months. Nine months, ha!

COR: I see. You just don't have the study facilities any more.

CEE: Study facilities! That's a joke! I move around the house all night, trying to find a place to study. There just isn't anyplace! And when I suggested I move out to the college in the dorm, my mother said no.

COR: I see.

CEE: They couldn't afford it, my mother said. That isn't the real reason, I know. The real reason is she doesn't trust me. She never has. She never could. She never would. It's not her nature. She's so-o-o suspicious.

COR: She doesn't feel she can trust you.

CEE: She wouldn't trust the Virgin Mary.

COR: She's a very suspicious woman.

CEE: And how!

[PAUSE.]

And I'm getting to be just like her.

COR: Tell me, how's that?

CEE: I keep thinking everybody doesn't like me, and I'm always picking on everybody. Probably that's why they don't — 'cause I'm always picking on them.

COR: You're always picking on everybody.

CEE: I pick on my father, and even my mother. I act like her, and then I hate myself for it.

COR: So you act like her.

CEE: Yeah.

COR: Yes. And what sort of brought all this to a head is that you can't seem to do what you think, uh, is "your" kind of work in school.

CEE: Uh, yes. I suppose so.

[PAUSE.]

Yeah. I go somewhere to study and I spend a half hour reading the same page. That's not right. I never used to do that .

COR: You can't seem to concentrate.

[PAUSE.]

CEE: Right. I can't seem to concentrate.

[PAUSE.]

Uh, I feel, well, uh, lazy, powerless, like I can't do anything about it.

COR: Sort of helpless.

CEE: Yeah, helpless. And afraid. I'm afraid. And I don't know what I'm afraid of. Crazy, huh?

COR: No-o. Many people have that feeling. Sort of afraid of you don't know what. Like fears of the unknown.

CEE: Yeah. I'm reading and all of a sudden I'm afraid. There's no reason for it. I'm just afraid.

[PAUSE.]

But I guess I really know why.

COR: Tell me.

CEE: It's all my mother. Her constant picking on me. It's that. I know. She picks on me like I can't do anything. She keeps telling me that, and I'm beginning to believe it. I'm beginning to believe it. After a while it gets to you, if you know what I mean.

COR: You feel she's come to make you feel inadequate.

CEE: Exactly. Inadequate. That's how I feel, and *she* did it to me. I didn't used to feel like that. I used to feel adequate, very adequate.

COR: And these feelings of inadequacy have developed only recently — is that it?

CEE: Uh, well, uh, I don't know.

[SILENCE.]

COR: You used to feel adequate. You don't know why you don't now.

CEE: Yeah, I guess.

[SILENCE.]

COR: You think less of yourself because of your mother's attitude toward you.

CEE: Yeah. That's what it is. My mother's picking on me because of, well, because of my aunt's coming to live with us. She's older than my mother. She never had any kids. Her husband died, and she came to live with us. And my mother gave her my room. So I haven't got any room. I haven't got my own closet, even! My stuff's all over the house. I'm living like a damned gypsy. That's what I am — I'm a gypsy. My mother calls me that all the time now, and she's right! She's turned me into a gypsy, and then she picks on me about it. God!

COR: So all this started when your aunt came to live with you.

CEE: Yeah, I guess.

COR: Before that your mother didn't pick on you.

CEE: Oh, she picked on me, I suppose. She's always picked on me. That gypsy business bothers me.

COR: You're living life out of a suitcase, is that it?

CEE: Worse than that. At least when you got a suitcase you have everything in one place, there. I haven't got any suitcase to keep things in. They're all over. In the living room, in my old room, my parents' room, in the dining room — all over. Sometimes when my mother doesn't lay things out for me, when that happens, sometimes I might have to go into my aunt's room or my parents' bedroom. It's all, all so embarrassing, if you know what I mean. I'm just under too much tension, tension, tension. It's all kind of crazy, if you know what I mean.

[PAUSE.]

I just don't like the set-up at home. I don't like the idea of being thrown out of my room. I don't like the idea of living like a gypsy. I don't like being at home. I don't like living there at all any more. I wish I could be free — away from all of them.

COR: You don't like being thrown out of your room, of living at home like a gypsy; you'd like to be independent.

CEE: Yes. That's right, yes. And really there's more to it than even that. See, I've tried to be a little independent, but they won't let me — they won't. It's mostly my mother, but my father's guilty, too. See, I'm working part-time, in a restaurant as a waitress. And I've been earning pretty good money, too. They didn't tell me I had to work. I wanted to — I guess it was so I could be, well, not free of them, I suppose, but just to do a few things, buy a few things . . . especially clothes for myself. My mother's never even let me buy my own clothes. Can you imagine that! Can you? She never trusted me. She never trusted me for anything. Not anything!

[PAUSE.]

COR: Uh, yes. You went to work part-time so you could, uh, do a few things for yourself, especially to buy clothes.

CEE: Right. And you know what?

COR: Tell me.

CEE: I had to fight for the right to do *that*.

COR: To buy your clothes after you earned the money?

CEE: Right. Can you imagine that? Can you? Honest. I swear, I feel like I'm swimming in molasses, upstream, to get the most ordinary things!

COR: That's quite graphic! (*Chuckle.*)

CEE: I do —

COR: H-m-m. (*Pause.*)

Your mother wouldn't let you pick out your own clothes.

CEE: Yeah.

COR: This really bothered you.

CEE: Yeah.

COR: Why do you suppose —

CEE: It's like everything else that happened all my life. She told me that I had the taste of a child. That my taste was no good, or that I just have no taste.

COR: I see.

CEE: No wonder I got problems! You get to believe it after a while. I have no confidence. I'm afraid to try new things, like tennis for instance.

COR: Tennis?

CEE: A lot of my friends have taken up tennis.

COR: But not you.

CEE: Right. Why? Because I just don't want to go through that period where people see I can't do it. I just don't want to go through that period when I'm learning.

COR: You're afraid to try new things.

CEE: Right.

COR: You don't like to be criticized.

CEE: Right.

COR: You feel you get enough at home.

CEE: Exactly.

[PAUSE.]

See, the problem is that I never had a mother who did a thing for me. I mean, in the right sense.

COR: You felt you never had a mother who was interested in you for yourself.

CEE: Right. She never loved me just because I'm me. She loved me, uh, only if I, uh, made her feel proud. Like if I, uh, if I got all A's in school or if I got some prize, like the debating prize. I won the debating prize every year I was in high school.

COR: You liked to debate.

CEE: I hated it. I hated it with a passion. I was terrified to get up in front of half the town to debate. I just don't like being the center of attention.

COR: You don't like being the center of attention, but you did it to please your mother.

CEE: Right. All through school from kindergarten. (*Pause.*) We lived next door to some people who moved, thank God. Anyway, they had a girl who is only four days older than me. Well, this girl's mother is exactly like my mother. Two beauts! Both of them were always bragging about us — who was prettier, smarter, more popular, you name it.

Cor: It was hard growing up under those circumstances.

Cee: It was hell. It was awful.

Cor: You always tried very hard, so your mother would be proud of you.

Cee: Yeah, so she could brag about me to Mrs. Williams next door. I remember so clearly. I couldn't have been more than six, maybe seven. I was sitting on my mother's lap and Dorie Williams was on her mother's. And Mrs. Williams said something like, "Dorie's teacher thinks she's the smartest one in the room." And my mother said, "Well, that teacher's a liar, or two-faced, or both!" (To my mother everybody is a "liar, or two-faced, or both.") She said, "Because she told *me* that Mary is the brightest child she's ever had." Well, maybe the teacher told her that. I don't know. But I got a feeling *she* was the one who was lying.

Cor: That incident made quite an impression on you.

Cee: Yeah, it did. I don't know why — Well, I guess I really do. All my life I had Dorie Williams as my rival. She was my rival all my life. I didn't want her as my rival, I wanted her as my friend. She was the only kid on my street who was my age. I was lonely, so often, because I'd fight with her. I'd fight with her only because I learned to hate her. Yes, I guess I learned to hate her because she was my rival. She was trying to beat me out, and I was trying to beat her out. All because of our stupid mothers, we both learned to hate each other. They moved away to another state about a month after we graduated from high school. I wonder if she'll remember me with any pleasant feelings? I doubt it. Stupid mothers.

[Pause.]

Cor: You wish you could have had a more pleasant relationship with Dorie Williams.

Cee: Yeah, I do. And the way I see it — It was my mother who did that to me, who took and made Dorie my rival instead of my friend. I never had many friends. None of them were good enough for me, or so my mother said. She picked on them, criticized them. She'd ask them the most personal questions. God, they embarrassed me. Like, "What nationality are your grandparents?" And once she asked a girl how much money her father made, 'cause she got a car for a graduation present. Isn't that awful?

Cor: These questions embarrassed you.

Cee: Mother spent most of her life embarrassing me. Once when I was in the third grade she came to school to talk with the teacher and ended up calling her a "misfit." I remember 'cause it was the first time that I had ever heard the word. It made quite an impression on me. Whenever I hear that word I think of Miss Connor and how embarrassed she was made by my mother, right there in front of the whole class. God, I could have died for her, and for me, too!

Cor: You were embarrassed as much as she was.

Cee: I'll say. But I guess I knew it was going to happen, because I dreaded her coming to school. I guess I knew my mother already. She always assumes people are trying to take advantage of her. I just don't go shopping with her. I stopped when I was thirteen. It's just more than I can take. She fights with every other sales girl. And the scenes in the restaurants! She figures the silverware's always dirty. Even if it looks clean she wipes each piece of silverware. She's always making the waitresses take back dishes, food, and anything else.

Cor: You're embarrassed to go out with her.

Cee: Yes, I am.

Cor: I see.

Cee: She's so suspicious. She trusts nobody, not me, not my aunt, not my father. I'll bet she doesn't even trust herself!

[Pause.]

She's so suspicious she checks the gas tank when I get home to see how many miles I drove. She always wants me in the house by midnight. I'm a big girl now! I mean, for heaven's sake!

Cor: Her suspicious ways upset you. You feel you should be permitted more —

Cee: Freedom. Or at least be treated like a person my age should be treated. She makes me so-o-o angry. I feel so helpless when she gets like that. I can't study, I can't do anything. Nothing.

Cor: You can't study. (*Pause.*) The problem centers around your mother.

Cee: Well, yeah. But I figure it's me, too.

Cor: You too?

Cee: Yeah, me.

Cor: How do you figure you're the problem?

(*Client starts to cry.*)

[Silence.]

Cee: It's a long story. Too long to tell here.

[Pause.]

God. How could it happen! God —

Cor: (*Handing counselee some Kleenex*) It will be all right, Mary.

Cee: Not this. This won't. Nobody can fix this. Nobody. Nothing can help me.

Cor: You feel like you're beyond help.

Cee: Yeah. I am.

Cor: You're here though.

Cee: (*Bursts into tears again.*) Oh, God!

[Pause.]

Cor: Apparently, whatever the difficulty is, it affects others.

Cee: That's it exactly. It isn't just myself I'm worried about, it's really not that so much. It's what they'll think when they find out.

[Pause.]

Cor: Your parents?

CEE: Who else?

COR: You're afraid of their reaction to —

CEE: My pregnancy.

[PAUSE.]

COR: You're pregnant.

CEE: Yeah, I am. (*Sighs.*)

COR: (*Sighs.*) I see.

CEE: And the thing that worries me the most is my mother.

[PAUSE.]

I don't feel ashamed for myself. But God, wait 'til she finds out! Wait 'til she finds out. Just wait!

[PAUSE.]

She'll have a kitten (chuckle) when she finds out that I'm going to have a baby. (*Pause.*) She'll just die.

COR: She'll be very upset.

CEE: And how!

COR: How do you feel about that?

[PAUSE.]

CEE: Scared, I suppose. Scared.

COR: Scared of how she's going to react to the news?

CEE: Yeah.

COR: What do you suppose she'll do, she'll say?

CEE: I don't know what she'll do, but there isn't much she won't say. I shudder just to think. See, this is going to confirm everything she's ever thought about me. It goes along with being a "gypsy" in her eyes.

COR: She thinks you're a tramp.

CEE: Exactly. (*Pause.*) This will confirm it for her. (*Pause.*) Anyway, I guess I am.

COR: You think you're a tramp.

CEE: Well, I'm pregnant and I'm not married. That makes me a tramp in everybody's eyes. It's the being pregnant that does it.

COR: It's the being pregnant that does it. That makes you a tramp in everybody's eyes.

CEE: Right. I know girls that have had relations six times a week and twice on Sunday, and nobody thinks a thing about it. They're even considered nice girls or sophisticated.

COR: I thought people believed that only the nice girls get caught.

CEE: Ha! Don't you believe it. If they believed that, they wouldn't have homes for unwed mothers.

[SILENCE.]

God! How could it happen to me? How? How could I do it to them?

COR: Your parents?

CEE: Yeah. Them. (*Pause.*) Wait till she finds out! Just wait. She and my aunt. The two of them will have a ball. They'll enjoy the misery of it all.

COR: Your mother and your aunt will enjoy the fact that you're pregnant.

CEE: Sounds crazy, huh?

COR: No, not crazy. I think I know what you mean. It goes along with what you were saying about how she kept seeing you as a tramp. I suppose it's part of the business of confirming her constant thoughts about you, her suspicions of you, I suppose.

CEE: Right. (*Bitterly.*) Serves her right.

COR: You probably feel that those suspicions of hers had something to do with your getting pregnant.

CEE: A lot. A real lot. She kept telling me I was a gypsy, so I finally went and did it.

COR: Did it?

CEE: Showed her *I am.*

COR: You feel you're a tr————, a, uh, gypsy.

CEE: The word's tramp. You were right the first time.

COR: You feel you're a tramp.

CEE: I don't know what I am.

[SILENCE.]

COR: You don't know what you are.

CEE: (*Sighs.*) (*Weeping.*) Oh, what does it matter? I know one thing — I'm pregnant.

COR: This is the only thing you can think about.

CEE: Right, it is.

COR: This is why you're not doing well in school.

CEE: Right. That's why. (*Pause.*) Studying is easy. My problem isn't. My problem's being pregnant, with my mother.

COR: Your mother's reaction is what, uh, really scares you.

CEE: Yeah, and the fact that she's got my aunt to worry about it all with.

COR: I see.

[PAUSE.]

CEE: It's her and my aunt. (*Pause.*) Not my father.

COR: Your father's reaction doesn't trouble you, at least not as much.

CEE: Well, yes and no. Actually, I feel worst of all about him. He's going to be hurt, I suppose; really hurt. He's really a good man, a real nice guy. (*Sighs.*) If I feel bad for anybody it's him. No, he won't say much, but I know him. He'll be really hurt by it all. He won't say much, but he'll probably want to die when he hears about it all.

COR: He'll kind of suffer in silence.

CEE: Yeah, he'll do that. He's been doing that for — uh, for ever since he's known my mother. (*Pause.*) He's a martyr, I swear, that's what he is.

COR: He's had a tough life with your mother.

CEE: Yeah. (*Sighs.*) He got caught in the middle.

COR: How do you mean, "Caught in the middle?"

CEE: Well, he got in the middle between me and my mother, uh, her treating me like I'm a tramp and me showing her I am, a, a, tramp.

COR: Yes. And you feel like he will be the one who will be hurt the most because of it all.

CEE: Right. And he'll show it the least. My mother, fed by my aunt, will carry on like an actress. "Oh, Mary, how could you do this to *me*," — That's her favorite line. "How could you do this to *me*." Everything I do, every blessed thing I do, is always seen as in relation to her, how it's going to affect her. God! (*Pause.*) Wait 'til she finds out who the father is! Ha!

COR: She knows the father.

CEE: She sure does. I've been going with only one boy ever since I ever dated.

COR: I take it she doesn't like him.

CEE: Can't stand him.

COR: She doesn't like him.

CEE: Not even a little bit.

COR: How do you feel about him?

CEE: He's all right.

COR: All right?

[PAUSE.]

CEE: Well, he's just like my mother. He even looks like her a little.

COR: He's like her.

CEE: Yeah. He's got the same kind of temperament. He picks at me like she does. I can't ever satisfy him, no matter what I do, no matter how hard I try. He makes me feel like *she* does, like I can't ever do anything right. They're two of a kind, I suppose.

COR: They're alike in that they make impossible demands on you.

CEE: Yeah; and they pick at me, making me feel like I'm a nothing.

COR: They both lower your self-esteem.

CEE: Yeah, they do that. (*Pause.*) They're so much alike you'd think they'd like each other. They don't. She calls him the local town bum.

COR: She calls him a bum.

CEE: Yeah. (*Pause.*) And I suppose he is. He's one of those who wears his hair long and doesn't shave regularly.

COR: Hm-m-m-m.

CEE: And he doesn't have a job, I mean a regular job.

COR: He doesn't go to school.

CEE: No. He went one semester to college and quit. (*Chuckle.*) He quit before they notified him that he'd flunk out. He gets so much pleasure out of telling me and everybody else that. He always wants to feel that he determines everything for himself.

COR: He wants to feel like he's the boss.

CEE: Yeah. But he'll never be the boss of anything. — He's just too, too angry at the world.

COR: He's a, uh, I suppose you'd term him a "rebel."

CEE: He's that all right. And he's also very much alone. That's why I find him attractive.

COR: Because he's alone?

CEE: Yeah. He's completely and utterly alone. Nobody likes him. Everybody makes fun of him. He needs somebody, badly.

COR: He needs you.

CEE: It happens to be me.

COR: It could be anybody else.

CEE: Yeah. But I happened to be around. (*Pause.*) He's so, so, incompetent.

COR: He's incompetent?

CEE: Yeah. That's why, that and the hair and beard — and he's not the cleanest boy — that's why my mother hates him.

COR: She hates him.

CEE: Yeah. But despite these qualities he's like her, too.

COR: How's that?

CEE: Well, he does about the most stupid things! Like once he left a newspaper in a restaurant, and he walked two miles back to get it, just 'cause he hadn't done the crossword puzzle in it. That's the kind of thing my mother would do. In fact, once she did it — only it was a magazine! He's like her about making scenes, too. Like he'll start a fight whenever anybody makes a comment about his hair, and an awful lot of people do. He argues with almost everybody he buys things from. It seems like I'm almost always in the middle of a scene when I'm with him. I stopped going out with my mother because she always did that, and then I started with him! Sometimes I think I'm crazy!

COR: He does seemingly stupid things, and he seems to get you into the middle of a scene.

CEE: Yeah.

COR: You don't like it.

CEE: No.

COR: 'Cause it's what your mother might do.

CEE: Yeah. Plus I'm not that kind of person.

COR: You're not like your mother and your boyfriend.

CEE: God, no. I'm much more shy than they are.

COR: Yes. (*Pause.*)
You're more shy than they are.

CEE: That's one of the things I worry about.

COR: You worry about being shy.

CEE: Yeah, well I don't really worry about being shy. I just wonder what I'm going to do, what I'm going to look like, and how I'm going to face my mother six or seven months from now.

COR: This, uh, ah, wonder you think comes from the fact that basically you're a shy person.

CEE: Yes.

[PAUSE.]

This shyness — maybe it's fear, I don't know, I'm confused about all of it. Anyway, I haven't told Danny about it.

COR: Danny is your boy friend.

CEE: Yes.

COR: You haven't told him that you're pregnant.

CEE: No, I haven't. It will break him up, I know.

COR: What do you mean by "break him up"?

CEE: He'll get completely rattled. He won't know what to do about it. Ha! There really isn't much he can do, anyway. He'll probably feel like he's got to marry me. I don't want that. God, he might even go to work, to support the baby. In his own strange way he's quite a responsible person.

COR: You don't want to tell him because he won't know what to do about it, uh, because he'll want to marry you out of some sense of responsibility. He might feel like he'll have to work to support a family. He'll —

CEE: And he'll do it all out of a sense of responsibility and end up hating me and the baby, because he won't, uh, he won't be doing any of these things because he wants to; but just because he feels he has to. See?

COR: Yes, Mary. I see. You don't want to force him to do anything he doesn't want to. And you feel by telling him you're pregnant you will be forcing him through, uh, guilt, perhaps?

CEE: That's it. That's it. That's how I was treated all my life by my mother. She got me to do a lot of things by making me feel guilty. Danny's like that, too. He asks me to meet him. And I'll agree, but then I find I can't for some reason — usually my mother — and then he pouts and throws it up to me that I always break my promises. And I guess I do have to break a lot of them. But it's only because he badgers me into agreeing to do something that I usually know I can't do, or I know it's too hard to do easily. Am I making any sense to you?

COR: Yes. Yes. Somehow this constant guilt you carry seems to perpetuate itself by forcing you into promises you can't keep. And when you can't meet the promises you find yourself feeling guilty again.

CEE: Yes, you seem to understand. (*Pause.*) I'd like to know how I got this way — how, how'd I get involved with Danny?

COR: You said Danny's like your mother.

CEE: Yeah.

[SILENCE.]

COR: You want to know how you got involved with Danny.

CEE: Well, not only that, but why am I so shy with any other boy? Why can't I be like other people? I'd like to like other boys. I mean, and girls too. Everybody can be nice, too, I suppose, but I've never really thought so. I've never learned that they are. You know what I mean?

COR: Yes, I think so. You want to be able to like others, both boys and girls. You probably feel you've never learned that they are likeable, for some reason or another.

CEE: Oh, I know what the reason is! That reason is my mother. She brought me up with the idea that there's something wrong with everybody. (*Pause.*) When I was a little girl she used to say "Now Mary, I don't want you playing with those children," and she always wanted me in my own back yard.

COR: And this taught you that —

CEE: That there's something the matter with everybody. I don't want to believe that, but I'm beginning to. And that maybe there's something the matter with me. I'm beginning to believe that.

COR: Hm-m-m. You think there's something the matter with you?

CEE: Oh, I don't know. The truth is that at this point I don't know what's the matter with me. (*Chuckle.*) That's not true, either! I know "I'm with child," as the romantics say. But that's not the whole thing, either, even though I suppose that's what brought me here.

COR: There's something besides your pregnancy you're concerned about.

CEE: Yeah, me! I don't want to end up like my mother or like my aunt. They're so unhappy! They hate so much. They hate everybody, people, each other, and themselves most of all. I don't want that. Not even a little bit.

COR: You don't want to be like your aunt and your mother.

CEE: No, I don't. My aunt's a bitter old lady, and I can see why. God, who could love her! Not that she's not pretty, and I'm sure she was even more so when she was younger. But she's got such a sour attitude toward everything and everybody. She just doesn't like people.

COR: And you want to.

CEE: Yes, I do.

COR: I see. Yes. I think your time is up for today. Uh —

CEE: I'd like to see you again.

COR: Good. Let's make it for next week, in the morning if you can. And there are some usual procedural forms I wish you'd fill out. You can do it at the secretary's desk.

CEE: Thank you, Doctor. I'll see you next week.

COR: Good seeing you, Mary.

APPENDIX B

Counselor's Summary of Initial Interview

Date: 13 May, 196–

Name of Counselee: Mary Dolores Smith
Age: 19   Sex: F   Residence: 17 Beaumont Street, City
Expected date of graduation: June, 196–
Telephones: Home   586–0077   Dormitory: Other:
Referral by: self   Marital state: single
Date of marriage: Age of Spouse:
Occupation of spouse:

Additional Pertinent Information: I.Q. 128; high school rank: 9th in a class of 426; lives at home with parents and aunt; aunt recently moved in and displaced her from her room.

Manifest Problem (as presented by the counselee): Can't study, failing in two courses; acutely poor relations with her mother; CLIENT FINALLY ADMITTED WHY SHE CAME FOR COUNSELING — pregnancy.

Counselor Impressions: (Use additional sheets if necessary)
    See attached sheets. I found the client to be exceedingly anxious and tense. She had difficulty explaining her problem and for a time dealt only with two symptoms, namely poor academic work and difficulties at home. The home problems seem to center around her mother and her aunt, with her mother the apparent real culprit. Most of her problems with the aunt seem to stem from the fact that the latter has moved into her home and displaced her from her room. This displacement apparently reinforced and triggered off many old feelings that any love her mother may have had for

89

her was purely conditional. Mary has felt all her life that she had to "perform" if she was to be loved. "She never loved me just because I'm me. She loved me . . . only if I got all A's in school." Quite simply, Mary feels that all her life she has given to her mother and has received little in return.

Her constant contact with her mother has resulted in a host of unfortunate identifications: i.e., emotional, "I keep thinking everybody doesn't like me;" behavioral, "I'm always picking on everybody . . . I act like her;" perceptual, ". . . there's something the matter with everybody."

Mary is pregnant. The dynamics of the pregnancy are probably many and varied and, quite honestly, it is difficult to determine them clearly at this time. Right now my belief is that Mary got pregnant to show her mother that she (Mary), too, is a woman and not a child: "My mother never even let me buy my own clothes." Also, Mary had an emotional vengeful striving to prove her mother's hostile and belittling perception of her — that she is a tramp — a belief, unfortunately, which Mary, in part at least, has acquired. Mary may also have been releasing hostility or seeking to bring shame on her mother: "I don't feel that ashamed for myself. But God, wait 'till she finds out." Then, too, Mary sees a lot of her mother in the illegitimate father. ". . . he's just like my mother. He even looks like her a little." We may speculate that in attempting to please her boy friend by succumbing to his advances, she might in truth have been attempting to please her mother, a trait deeply ingrained. Consider this exchange, for example:

COR: You didn't like being the center of attention, but you did it to please you mother.
CEE: Right. All through school from kindergarten on —

Of course, there are other and even more obvious qualities in Mary. She is insecure and feels quite unloved. And these unsatisfied needs form the foundation for an acutely low self-esteem: "Exactly, inadequate. That's how I feel —. No wonder I got problems! You get to believe it after a while. I have no confidence. I'm afraid to try new things . . ."

And what are Mary's strengths? Mary is intelligent (I.Q., 128) and she uses her intelligence to advantage. Thus she intellectualizes and acquires cognitive understanding quickly. For example, toward the end of the interview Mary quickly deduced that her mother's requirement that she play in her own back yard was a strong contributing factor to her belief that ". . . there's something the matter with everybody . . . that there's something the matter with me."

Mary seeks to be emotionally independent. Her going out to work, for example, reflects this search for independence. She virtually states this, too:

COR: . . . You feel you should be permitted more —
CEE: Freedom. Or at least be treated like a person my age should be treated.

Mary is introspective and intellectually and emotionally curious. She seeks to understand her dynamics, for she states: "I'd like to know how I got this way . . . how I'd get involved with Danny."

But Mary's greatest asset probably is that she *wants* to change. She wants not only to perceive a friendlier world but also to interact more effectively in such a world. Thus she states: "Why can't I be like other people? I'd like to like other boys, I mean and girls, too. Everybody can be nice, too, I suppose."

I feel that the prognosis is good. Mary wants help. She referred herself; and, more important still, she asked for another interview.

BIBLIOGRAPHY

"A Report of the Committee on Professional Preparation and Standards; a Statement of Policy — the Counselor: Professional Preparation and Role." *Personality and Guidance*, Vol. XLI, No. 5, 1963, pp. 480–485.

Arbuckle, D. S., *Counseling: An Introduction*. Boston: Allyn and Bacon, Inc., 1961.

Bixenstine, V. E., and Page, H. A., "Case Report: On the Meaning of Symptoms." *Journal of Counseling Psychology*, Vol. 2, 1964, pp. 164–167.

Bordin, E. S., "The Implication of Client Expectations for the Counseling Process." *Journal of Counseling Psychology*, Vol. 2, 1955, pp. 17–21.

Buck, L. A., and Cuddy, J. M., "A Theory of Communication in Psychotherapy." *Psychotherapy: Theory, Research, and Practice*, Vol. 3, 1966, pp. 7–13.

Burton, A., "Beyond the Transference." *Psychotherapy: Theory, Research, and Practice*, Vol. I, 1964, pp. 49–53.

Canon, H. J., "Personality Variables and Counselor-Client Affect." *Journal of Counseling Psychology*, Vol. 1, 1964, pp. 35–41.

Carkhuff, R. R., and Truax, C. B., "Training in Counseling and Psychotherapy: an Evaluation of an Integrated Didactic and Experiential Approach." *Journal of Consulting Psychology*, Vol. 29, 1965, pp. 333–336.

Clemes, S. R., and D'Andrea, V. S., "Patients' Anxiety as a Function of Expectation and Degree of Initial Interview Anxiety." *Journal of Consulting Psychology*, Vol. 29, 1965, pp. 397–404.

Colby, K. M., *A Primer for Psychotherapists*. New York: The Ronald Press, 1951.

Ellsworth, S. G., "The Consistency of Counselor Feeling-Verbalization." *Journal of Counseling Psychology*, Vol. 10, 1963, pp. 356–361.

Freud, S., *Collected Papers, Vol II*. New York: Basic Books, 1959.

Grater, H. A., "Client Preferences for Affective or Cognitive Counselor Characteristics and First Interview Behavior." *Journal of Counseling Psychology*, Vol. 11, 1964, pp. 248–250.

Goodstein, L. D., and Grigg, A. E., "Client Satisfaction, Counselors and the Counseling Process." *Personnel and Guidance Journal*, Vol. 38, 1959, pp. 19–26.

Grigg, A. E., and Goodstein, L. D., "The Use of Clients as Judges of the

Counselor's Performance." *Journal of Counseling Psychology*, Vol. 4, 1957, pp. 31–36.

Hollon, T. H., and Zolik, E. S., "Self-Esteem and Symptomatic Complaints in the Initial Phase of Psychoanalytically Oriented Psychotherapy." *American Journal of Psychotherapy*, Vol. XVI, 1962, pp. 83–93.

Ingham, H. V., and Love, L. R., *The Process of Psychotherapy*. New York: McGraw Hill Book Co., 1954.

Kanfer, F. H., "Structure of Psychotherapy: Role Playing as a Variable in Dynamic Communication." *Journal of Consulting Psychology*, Vol. 29, 1965, pp. 325–332.

Kirk, B. A., "Counseling Phi Beta Kappas." *Journal of Counseling Psychology*, Vol. 2, 1955, pp. 304–307.

Lorr, M., "Client Perceptions of Therapists: A Study of the Therapeutic Relation." *Journal of Consulting Psychology*, Vol. 29, 1965, pp. 146–149.

McNair, D. M., Lorr, M., and Callahan, D. M., "Patient and Therapist Influence on Quitting Psychotherapy." *Journal of Consulting Psychology*, Vol. 27, 1963, pp. 10–17.

Maslow, A. H., and Mintz, N., "Effects of Esthetic Surroundings: Initial Short-Term Effects of Three Esthetic Conditions Upon Perceiving 'Energy' and 'Well-Being' in Faces." *Journal of Psychology*, Vol. 41, 1956, pp. 247–254.

Matarazzo, J. D., Saslow, G., Wiens, A. N., Weitman, M., and Allen, B. V., "Interviewer Head-Nodding and Interviewee Speech Durations." *Psychotherapy: Theory, Research, and Practice*, Vol. 1, 1964a, pp. 54–63.

Matarazzo, J. D., Wiens, A. N., Saslow, G., Allen, B. V., and Weitman, M., "Interviewer Mm-Hmm and Interviewee Speech Durations." *Psychotherapy: Theory, Research, and Practice*, Vol. 1, 1964b, pp. 109–115.

Mendelsohn, G. A., and Kirk, B. A., "Personality Differences Between Students Who Do and Do Not Use Counseling Facility." *Journal of Counseling Psychology*, Vol. 9, 1962, pp. 341–346.

Michaux, M. W., and Lorr, M., "Psychotherapists' Treatment Goals." *Journal of Counseling Psychology*, Vol. 8, 1961, pp. 250–254.

Mills, D. H., and Abeles, N., "Counselor Needs for Affiliation and Nurturance as Related to Liking for Clients and Counseling Process." *Journal of Counseling Psychology*, Vol. 12, 1965, pp. 353–358.

Mills, D. H., Chestnut, W. H., and Hartzell, J. P., "The Needs of Counselors: A Component Analysis." *Journal of Counseling Psychology*, Vol. 13, 1966, pp. 82–84.

Mintz, N. L., "Effects of Esthetic Surroundings: Prolonged and Repeated Experience in a 'Beautiful' and an Ugly Room." *Journal of Psychology*, Vol. 41, 1956, pp. 459–466.

Munson, J., "Patterns of Client Resistiveness and Counselor Response." *Dissertation Abstracts*, Vol. 21, 1961, pp. 2368–2369.

Olsen, L. C., "Religious Values and Counselor Fantasies." *The Journal of General Psychology*, Vol. 74, 1966, pp. 81–88.

Osgood, C. E., and Suci, G. J., *The Measurement of Meaning*. Urbana: University of Illinois Press, 1957.

Patterson, C. H., *Counseling and Psychotherapy: Theory and Practice*. New York: Harper and Row, 1959.

————, "Control, Conditioning, and Counseling." *Personnel and Guidance Journal*, Vol. XLI, 1963, pp. 680–685.

Pepinski, H. B., and Karst, T. O., "Convergence: A Phenomenon in Counseling and Psychotherapy." *American Psychologist*, Vol. 19, 1964, pp. 333–338.

Perez, Joseph F., *Counseling: Theory and Practice*. Reading, Massachusetts: Addison-Wesley, 1965.

Phillips, J. S., Matarazzo, R. G., Matarazzo, J. D., Saslow, G., and Kanfer, F. H., "Relationships Between Descriptive Content and Interaction Behavior in Interview." *Journal of Consulting Psychology*, Vol. 25, 1961, pp. 260–266.

Pohlman, E., "Changes in Client Preferences During Counseling." *Personnel and Guidance Journal*, Vol. XL, 1961, pp. 340–343.

————, and Robinson, F. P., "Client Reaction to Some Aspects of the Counseling Situation." *Personnel and Guidance Journal*, Vol. 38, 1960, pp. 546–551.

Poole, A., "Counselor Judgement and Counseling Evaluation." *Journal of Counseling Psychology*, Vol. 4, 1957, pp. 37–40.

Rice, L. N., "Therapist's Style of Participation and Case Outcome." *Journal of Consulting Psychology*, Vol. 29, 1965, pp. 155–160.

Rogers, C. R., *Client-Centered Therapy*. Boston: Houghton Mifflin Co., 1951.

————, "The Necessary and Sufficient Conditions of Therapeutic Personality Change." *Journal of Consulting Psychology*, Vol. 2, 1957, pp. 95–103.

————, *On Becoming a Person*. Boston: Houghton Mifflin Co., 1961.

Rudikoff, L. C., and Kirk, B. A., "Goals of Counseling: Mobilizing the Counselee." *Journal of Counseling Psychology*, Vol. 8, 1961, pp. 243–249.

Schwebel, M., Karr, L., and Slotkin, H., "Counselor Relationship Competence: A Unifying Concept Applied to Counselor Trainees." *Educational and Psychological Measurement*, Vol. 19, 1959, pp. 515–537.

Shoben, E. J., Jr., "The Counselor's Theory as a Personal Trait." *Personnel and Guidance Journal*, Vol. 40, 1962, pp. 617–621.

Sonne, T. R., and Goldman, L., "Preferences of Authoritarian and Equalitarian Personalities for Client-Centered and Eclectic Counseling." *Journal of Counseling Psychology*, Vol. 4, 1957, pp. 129–135.

Soper, D. W., and Combs, A. W., "The Helping Relationship as Seen by Teachers and Therapists." *Journal of Consulting Psychology*, Vol. 26, 1962, p. 288.

Stoler, N., "Client Likability: A Variable in the Study of Psychotherapy." *Journal of Consulting Psychology*, Vol. 27, 1963, pp. 175–178.

Strickland, B. R., and Crowne, D. P., "Need for Approval and the Premature Termination of Psychotherapy." *Journal of Consulting Psychology*, Vol. 27, 1963, pp. 95–101.

Strupp, H. H., "A Multidimensional Comparison of Therapist Activity in Analytic and Client-Centered Therapy." *Journal of Consulting Psychology*, Vol. 21, 1957, p. 307.

Sullivan, H. S., *The Psychiatric Interview*. New York: W. W. Norton, 1954.

Tarachow, S., *An Introduction to Psychotherapy*. New York: International Universities Press, Inc., 1963.

Thompson, D. F., and Meltzer, L. F., "Communication of Emotional Intent by Facial Expression." *Journal of Abnormal and Social Psychology*, Vol. 68, 1964, pp. 129–135.

Thorne, F. C., "Principles of Personality Counseling: An Eclectic Viewpoint." *Journal of Clinical Psychology*, Vol. 124, No. 11, 1950, pp. 11, 121.

Tolbert, E. L., *Introduction to Counseling*. New York: McGraw Hill Book Co., 1959.

Tyler, L. E., "The Initial Interview." *Personnel and Guidance Journal*, Vol. 34, April, 1956, pp. 466–477.

Van der Veen, F., "Effects of the Therapist and the Patient on Each Other's Therapeutic Behavior." *Journal of Consulting Psychology*, Vol. 29, 1965, pp. 19–26.

————, and Stoler, N., "Therapist Judgements, Interview Behavior, and Case Outcome." *Psychotherapy: Theory, Research, and Practice*, Vol. 2, 1965, pp. 158–163.

Wallach, M. S., and Strupp, H. H., "Psychotherapists' Clinical Judgements and Attitudes Toward Patients." *Journal of Consulting Psychology*, Vol. 24, 1960, pp. 316–323.

Waskow, I. E., "Counselor Attitudes and Client Behavior." *Journal of Consulting Psychology*, Vol. 27, 1963, pp. 405–412.

Weitz, H., "Guidance and Behavior Change." *Personnel and Guidance Journal*, Vol. 89, 1961, p. 559.

Williamson, E. G., *Counseling Adolescents*. New York: McGraw-Hill Book Co., 1950.

————, "The Meaning of Communication in Counseling." *Personnel and Guidance Journal*, Vol. 36, 1959, p. 6.

————, "The Counselor as a Technique." *Personnel and Guidance Journal*, Vol. 41, 1962, pp. 108–111.

————, "Value Options and the Counseling Relationship." *Personnel and Guidance Journal*, Vol. 44, 1966, pp. 617–623.

Wolberg, L. R., *The Technique of Psychotherapy*. New York: Grune and Stratton, 1954.

Wrenn, R. L., "Counselor Orientation: Theoretical or Situational." *Journal of Counseling Psychology*, Vol. 7, 1960, pp. 40–45.

ANNOTATED BIBLIOGRAPHY

Arbuckle, D. S., *Counseling: An Introduction*. Boston: Allyn and Bacon, Inc., 1961.

Of particular interest to the reader of this monograph is Chapter 7, which presents the non-directive viewpoint on preparations for the initial contact and the establishment of rapport.

Erickson, E. E., *The Counseling Interview*. Englewood Cliffs, New Jersey: Prentice Hall, Inc., 1950.

Chapters 3 and 4 give the reader practical suggestions and insights on how to get the interview started.

Hahn, M. E., and MacLean, M., *Counseling Psychology*, 2nd ed. New York: McGraw Hill Book Company, 1955.

In chapter 10 the authors present a very systematic and thoughtful outline with which to assess an interview.

Patterson, C. H., *Counseling and Psychotherapy: Theory and Practice*. New York: Harper and Row, 1955.

Chapter 8, particularly pages 162–166. This considers the dynamics and anxiety attached to rapport for the counseling participants and is a very readable text.

Perez, J. F., *Counseling: Theory and Practice*. Reading, Massachusetts: Addison-Wesley, 1965.

Chapters 2, 3, and 4 expand on most of the points considered in this monograph.

Tolbert, E. L., *Introduction to Counseling*. New York: McGraw-Hill Book Company, 1959.

Chapter 2 illustrates an initial interview and then analyzes it.

Tyler, L. E., *The Work of the Counselor*, 2nd ed. New York: Appleton-Century-Crofts, Inc., 1961.

Chapter 3 considers both client and counselor attributes and expectations. Also included in this chapter are the author's thoughts on the goals of the initial interview.

Warters, J., *Techniques of Counseling*, 2nd ed. New York: McGraw-Hill Book Company, 1964.

Chapter 18 contains information which the student of the initial interview will find valuable. Pp. 413–421 will be of particular interest to the prospective and new counselor.

INDEX